CW01510883

CHILDSCOURT

John Coleman

Foreword by Nigel Whiskin

New European Publications London

First published by Macdonald & Co in 1967

Published in the United Kingdom in 2004 by

New European Publication
14-16 Carroun Road
London SW8 1JT, England

British Library Cataloguing in Publication Data

ISBN 1-872410-46-4

Printed and bound in Great Britain by CLE Print Limited, St Ives, Cambs.

NEW INTRODUCTION

By John Coleman

Childscourt was first published by Macdonald in 1968. Sadly it was a time when smaller publishers were being taken over by large international groups who tended to remainder any books not already on the international best seller lists. E.F. Schumacher's message, *Small is Beautiful*, had not yet permeated the thinking of these groups.

Although *Childscourt* had had some excellent reviews and was on the reading lists of many universities' departments of education, it was remaindered almost as soon as it came out. This was galling for me as I had hoped that I might have produced a useful record of the work of Bill Malcolm for future generations. Instead it lapsed into obscurity. Since those days however, a different and more violent social climate has developed. When I wrote it it seemed appropriate for the field of education. Now, with concern about crime in local communities and how it is spreading down the age groups even to teenagers and younger children, the emphasis has to be how we can tackle crime in today's context. Bill Malcolm's message must surely contribute to the answer.

It so happened that I received an invitation from Michael Hastings to Nigel Whiskin's retirement party. He'd been Chief Executive of Crime Concern for fourteen years and I knew as soon as I heard him speak that he was Bill Malcolm's kind of man. So when the opportunity occurred I asked if he'd write a foreword. I got an immediate and positive response. I said I would send him the book. Of course I knew if he found it awful he could change his mind, but having heard him speak I didn't worry about that. Instead I read the last page of the little booklet prepared for his party entitled 'Whiskin's Words of Wisdom', and decided to slip it in at the end of this book.

FOREWORD

By Nigel Whiskin

During the time John Coleman was writing the story of Bill Malcolm's development of *Childscourt*, I was in an Approved School in the Home Counties, doing the residential part of my training as a 'mature' entrant into the Probation Service. This residential experience nearly finished my career before it had begun; partly because the staff team were so deeply hostile not just to outsiders like me but also the young men in their care; partly because of the repressive and aggressive atmosphere of the institution that was about trying to make everyone conform to a regime that existed for no other reason than that it existed; partly the physical and emotional bullying by staff on staff, staff on young people, young people on young people, and young people on the staff.

Most of all it brought back memories of the first three years I spent as a boarder at a minor public school, the mostly deeply unhappy experience of my life. We lived in complete fear all the time. Fear of being punished by cane, slipper or detention if we talked out of turn, if we didn't turn our beds, failed our fagging duties, were caught eating in the street, wore the wrong clothes, if we did not conform to all the written and unwritten rules – many of which seemed to be made up on the spot. We were expected to die for the House, honour the Old Boys and cherish the name and the fame of the School. There was little or no space to grow as an individual and the worry of it was that after three years they almost won!

By the time I got to do the residential training I was married with two stepchildren and two of my own. I had read about A.S Neil and Summerhill, The Child, Family and the Outside World and the wonderful Dr Benjamin Spock. I was discovering that being a parent was just about the most difficult job anyone can expect to do in a lifetime. Everything that was going on in the Approved School went against the grain of both my experience and reading and the insights that came from both.

In telling Bill Malcolm's story of working with children and young people from difficult backgrounds, John Coleman for me rings the bells of some interrelated universal truths, as relevant now as they were then, forty years or more ago.

The first is that the only discipline that is worth striving for is self-discipline. I have been very impressed over many years now by the work Hy-Scope Perry Preschool, who have structured their educational activities with three to five year olds round a model of 'Plan, Do, Review.' The results in terms of giving children a better start to their educational careers and consequently setting them up to succeed in life are stunning. School failure is the single most significant indicator of a future criminal career that we can do something about – parents and siblings with criminal records, poor early parenting and erratic disciplining, growing up in a poor neighbourhood are in the 'there and then' category, they have happened and cannot be changed only ameliorated by casework interventions. We **can** help with education and training.

The second universal truth to emerge from *Childscourt* is about enabling children and young people to be a part of, and have influence over, their environment be it home, community or school. Gaining the confidence to challenge behaviours, by adults in authority as well as peers, is an invaluable life skill. Taking part in setting the community agenda, standards of behaviour, and establishing realistic ground rules is the highway to creating an environment in which all can flourish as individuals and as fully paid up members of the wider community.

For me, the third *Childscourt* lesson, so obvious but so important to always have in mind, is that children and young people learn how to treat one another by how they themselves are treated. Most social behaviour is learned by direct experience and by observation. We only have to look at domestic violence and sexual abuse cases to see how the abused and those who witness the abuses often become abusers themselves later on.

Most of my casework training, listening with the third ear, trying to attribute motives to people's behaviours, gaining insights and understanding about my 'clients', was derived from psychoanalytical theory and probably more use to me than the client group. Most of the people on my probation officer caseload came from poor backgrounds in poor neighbourhoods. Most needed practical help to survive, claim benefits, access to medical and dental care, find work and somewhere to live and deal with addiction problems. Most wanted to change their lives but lacked the self-belief and confidence to do so.

On a visit to a local prison, one young man told me there were three kinds of people in the nick; the mad, the bad and the sad. I met in the course of thirty-five years work with offenders only a few really bad and mad people, most were sad.

The enduring lesson from John Coleman's account of Bill Malcolm and *Childscourt* is about how commonsense, practical care and a kind of unending rough love can help so many sad children and young people find their true selves.

With a record prison population, with one in four young men acquiring a criminal record by their eighteenth birthday and with so many children and young people living in institutions, we in Britain need to heed the *Childscourt* lessons. Times and fashions change but without a lot of practical common sense support and unending rough love we cannot hope to enable our children and young people find ways out of crime and highways to a good and rewarding life.

Nigel Whiskin

Acknowledgements

The author and the publishers wish to thank the following people for permission to quote from correspondence or reports written personally, or officially by themselves or their predecessors in office on behalf of the organisations they represent:

Miss G. M. Aves, former Chief Welfare Officer, Ministry of Health;

Mr. D. M. Evans, Clerk to Gwyrfai Rural District Council;

Mr. D. W. T. Jenkins, former Director of Education, Caernarvonshire;

Dr. D. E. Perry-Pritchard, County Medical Officer of Health, Caernarvonshire;

Mr. A. F. Philp, Secretary, Family Service Units;

Mr. Tom Stephens, member of the Liverpool and District Pacifist Service Unit;

Mr. Mansel Williams, Director of Education, Caernarvonshire;

Miss E. Pentir Williams, former County Welfare Organiser, Caernarvonshire.

The author wishes especially to thank Mr. and Mrs. A. W. Malcolm for continuous and active help at all stages of the writing of this book and for allowing liberal quotation in it from their personal journals and memoranda. He is also most grateful to Mrs. Pat Goldacre, Head Teacher of Childscourt, for supplying a full and detailed account of the present running of the school. In addition his thanks are due to various present and past members of the staff who helped

Mr. Malcolm in the compilation of material for certain portions of his journals and memoranda quoted from in this book.

Finally, the author and the publishers would like to thank MacGibbon and Kee Ltd. and Mr. Michael Foot, the author of *Aneurin Bevan*, *Vol. 1*, for permission to reproduce an extract from that work.

Contents

7

It is part of a more refined humanity to have reverence 'for the mask,' and not make use of psychology and curiosity in the wrong place.

F. Nietzsche

Introduction

I hope that my account of the work of Bill Malcolm which culminated at Childscourt may help to illustrate that there is a way of being a teacher which steers between the Scylla of the old hard, but still quite deeply rooted traditional way and the Charybdis of a perhaps too permissive progressive ideal, and that this should be sought by all teachers for whom teaching is a true vocation.

Writing of one's own experience has always seemed to me to be a desperate and difficult task and I have wanted to echo the comment of William James that every book he wrote was accompanied by "groans and lamentations and vows to heaven that I would never do it again." Writing of another's experience is in a sense a double agony. In my case at any rate I have to feel a pressing need—an inevitability about the task—before I undertake it.

The story of Bill Malcolm's work at Childscourt and before is basically a fairly simple story but it contains an urgent message, more accurately several messages, to what in some ways appears a misled age, an age that has become terribly conscious of what it is doing with itself. This age has gained a wealth of possessions and new powers but it often tends to replace a wisdom that in former times was almost deliberately kept out of the glare of too conscious attention, with an over-conscious psychology.

Primarily, I feel that Childscourt has a message for those dealing with the problems of wayward youth. Certainly it has a message for those teachers who are sensitive to their work and to their children, and who wish to be genuinely progressive but who feel that they are being battered into cynicism not only by the practical demands of the system and the harshness of a few of their fellow teachers but even by the children towards whom they wish to be at least human. Must such people really be driven into behaving like the old brutal type of schoolteacher, even while paying lip-service to modern ideas? Perhaps the book has a special message for the kind of teacher who on occasion may hit out in desperation but whose deepest feelings are against doing so.

In addition, the story of the school contains an interesting and provocative message for the child psychiatrist and the educational psychologist. This is twofold. Firstly, it warns him of the image he is creating of himself among ordinary people who lack the intellectual sophistication to isolate the procedures and cures of psychiatry from the thought of themselves as mentally sick. Some unexpected side-effects of this seem to me to be highlighted in a most interesting way in Bill Malcolm's work and experiences. Secondly, it cautions him to be wary of being too ready to put children into the category of mentally sick, maladjusted, emotionally disturbed or whatever the prevailing term happens to be. In this connection, it is worth recalling one of Barbara Wootton's speeches on the Mental Health Bill in the House of Lords (Hansard, 4.7.62) where she referred to a remarkable book by Thomas Szasz, *The Myth of Mental Illness*. There Szasz tries to show that a great deal of what is recorded as mental illness is in fact an unconscious but stringent protest against actual conditions of life. In reading about Bill Malcolm's sometimes savage outbursts against psychology and psychiatry, it is necessary to bear in mind the strong feelings he has against extending the categories of mental illness beyond what he deems to be their proper limits. Szasz showed very clearly that certain symptoms which men in the army developed were not indications of mental disease but forms of unconscious protest, to which they were driven, against the actual conditions of military life. Those men were not psychological cases.

To read Bill Malcolm's story sympathetically one must realize from the outset that in a very deep and almost passionate way he felt the same about most of the children who were sent to him. Their protest was right. At the same time he knew that they needed insight into what was happening to them. He knew that their protest needed to be changed from a blind into an aware, purposeful protest. To him their protest was almost a sign of mental health. To some his rejection of prevailing interpretations of behaviour seemed totally unreasonable and verged on pig-headedness. To me, however, it seemed to be a way of thinking that came from deep down inside him, that communicated itself automatically to rejected children and that played no small part in his exceptional success with them.

His work also raises many important questions about conditions and relationships in our schools as well as in our homes. It is too easy to put all the blame on the home, as some educational psychologists do, while failing to look adequately at the true weaknesses in our educational system, particularly those in our sometimes scandalous Secondary Modern schools. At the time when a change-over to comprehensive education is more than just in the air it is surely important that all concerned should try hard to avoid carrying over any of the deeply ground-in faults of the old system into the new. It is because they highlight the results of some of these faults that the accounts of children who have been with the Malcolms may prove especially interesting to certain administrators in education.

The harmful emotional effects of low academic grading have recently been realized. Bill Malcolm has done much to show the catastrophic emotional effects of low *emotional* grading. Many schools are still far too unhappy places to compensate for the misery of bad homes. There is still too much savagery in hidden corners of the playground, too much bullying to which teachers turn a blind eye, too much punishment without an understanding of the particular cause of the offence, and above all too much cold distant punishment meted out according to Local Authority regulations. Children can understand a man who belts them in a moment of anger. He does not put himself on a higher plane of existence like the man who administers cold but accurate justice. I hope the story of Childscourt will help to illustrate this—really no more than the common-sense point of view—and to show how certain differences which can be brought about in the structure of the school society can have a momentous effect on the lives of many misunderstood children.

A recent story of an architect chatting to a schoolboy about the plans he was drawing up for his new school is not atypical, even if untrue. When asked how he liked the plans the boy replied, "If it was a marble palace it would still be bloody school!" It is obviously adults who, in spite of themselves, somehow make school what it is for children. Surely we must not be satisfied until we know that the majority of children go home at the end of the day with a sense of achievement and pleasure and end their schooldays with a growing desire for more education, simply because it is good.

The widespread fault in many schools may, I believe, be summed up in one word, alienation. In describing the hostility which arose between the mill owners and their workers in the North of England in the last century Karl Marx coined this remarkably appropriate term. Today it is often used without those tough associations, but with them, in varying degrees, I think it describes well the false relationship between teachers and children that exists throughout much of our state educational system. It was alienation that made the boy say, "it would still be bloody school".

The idea that our schooldays were the happiest days of our lives is now a discredited myth—an exaggeration that makes us suspicious that they might really have been the reverse. Most people express more honestly some sense of relief that that time is over and they have got away from "being bossed around by teachers". Childscourt has taken children who have already been excessively affected by this system and changed them. That is the mark of its value and the reason for its interest to all who care about children and their education.

An Unconventional
Entry into an Educational Career

If there is one thing that stands out more than anything else on the scene at Childscourt School, it is the absence of any trace of 'alienation' between the children and the staff. There is no sign that the children regard the staff in any sense as 'them'. It is truly *one* school. I believe that this springs from Bill Malcolm's own personal attitudes as principal, and that these have grown out of his own particular background. A brief biographical sketch will help to show the factors which went into the making of a successful school of this kind. It will show also how certain accidental factors operated in his case and led him towards a course which on his own account he would certainly have been disinclined to follow. I think it may suggest that the best people for staffing schools for difficult children, or dealing with difficult children within normal schools, may well be found outside traditional educational spheres and that some deliberate encouragement may be needed to get such people into the work.

Like many others who have been successful in life but failed to shine at school, Bill remembers his early days as being on the whole painful and unpleasant. School made an impact upon him that might in the ordinary course of events have turned him completely away from anything to do with schools and education and yet he says of it himself now: "I suppose the idea for the sort of school we have now was really born in my mind when kicking an old can around on the broken paving stones of a miserable little council school in Derbyshire many years ago. I was suddenly struck by the vile, drab surroundings, the colourless class-rooms, a horror of the teachers who seemed like cold tyrants from a different world, the sudden violence of some of the older kids and the general torture of it all. We were forced to learn tricks, which were not any recognized part of education, in order to survive."

It was a bitter experience and although forgotten about at the time, because of his involvement in games and other interests at home, it certainly created an indelible outline in Bill's mind of what a school should *not* be like. It also left an image of what he is inclined to imagine all other schools are like today. We know that there have been many external changes in the nature of schools and educa-tion, many genuine improvements, but much of it unfortun-ately is only papering over the cracks and ugly patches. The underlying unconscious attitudes to education are still the same. The responses of children are generally the same. It's still 'bloody school'. In due course Bill left school and was deeply affected by the misery he witnessed during the 1926 depression at an age when a young man's social ideals are being formed. A little later he emigrated to Australia.

In Australia he tried his fortune for almost twelve years, sometimes out on the stations and sometimes with unusual and highly unconventional people in the cities. It was a tough life but it was fought out on equal terms with his fellows. It had a kind of Wild West flavour about it which he was later peculiarly able to bring into school life. At times he stayed in the notorious Sydney Sailors' Home where he came up against some of the toughest down-and-outs it was possible to imagine meeting anywhere in the world, a place where the ideal of turning the other cheek could not be sustained for long. In Sydney he also spent some time with a family of artists whose morals and culture shook to the foundations the Christian precepts he had learnt at home.

All in all it was twelve years of harsh experience of human nature in the raw and he emerged with his deepest

14

convictions strengthened but with the dross of idealism discarded. There is a mystique in the understanding of human relations which is learnt among men out in pioneer countries beyond the protection of the law and the police, and this mystique is something to which children and adolescents seem to have an almost instinctive response. Bill was able to bring this back with him. During the last couple of years in Australia he had felt an irrepressible yearning to return home. He had spent those years as a working maintenance man in a convent quietly saving a portion of his wages to buy a passage on the boat to England.

Shortly after his return he married the daughter of a school teacher and settled down for a short time in a little cottage on the rocky coast of Cornwall near Lindsey Cove. War broke out soon after his marriage and one of the first results of this was that he and his wife, Lillian, found two evacuee children allocated to them. Billy and Tom, aged ten and twelve respectively, became the two new boisterous members of their family before they had had time to have any children of their own. They had collected them from the reception centre in Redruth, where children rushed out of London and torn from their parents were herded together like cattle in the large hall. Bill wondered how many of them would be sent to homes where they would be felt as intruders and expected to show gratitude for every small mercy. He wondered then, but not in words explicit even to himself, how many of them would become 'difficult' children. He identified himself with their feelings. Children thus uprooted could scarcely feel gratitude. Their basic feeling was bound to be that somehow the adult community had failed them.

One night Billy and Tom burst into the sitting room dressed as pirates. They said they'd found their gear in a box they'd fished out of a dried up well at the bottom of the garden. Both Bill and Lillian were obviously highly suspicious, but it was a remotely possible story. The cottage was over four hundred years old and a lot of smuggling had gone on there in previous centuries. Bill suggested that they should hang their find up on the wall and their readiness to do so helped to quell suspicion for the time being.

One evening, however, several days later, some friends were visiting Bill and Lillian in the cottage and asked where the pirates' gear had come from. Did they know that the hut belonging to the local Freemasons had been raided and some pirates' gear stolen from it and that the local police were scouring the area? Instantly Bill called the boys and told them that he knew where the clothes on the wall had come from. He said nothing against them but told them to go as quickly as possible under the cover of darkness and return the clothes. Relieved that Bill hadn't subjected them to a moral lecture on stealing, the boys hustled the clothes into bags and went off as Bill had suggested. The police search was called off when it was found that the missing things had been returned.

The boys got into one or two more scrapes, but with the help of sympathetic local inhabitants Bill always managed to rescue them and to persuade everybody that they were just normal boys a little disturbed by the troubles war had brought upon them. In a very short time they did indeed become just normal kids. They settled down well and no longer played the kind of games that brought them into trouble. Lillian then was the only one they bothered. Every spare hour of the day they needed something: scissors and string, pieces of wood and cloth. They climbed trees, they played Red Indians and engaged in war games with their friends, but they kept out of real bother. Bill had understood them. He had been on their side even when they were stealing and he had controlled them until they were strong enough and wise enough to control themselves. If he had taken any other course at that early stage their little escapades would certainly have snowballed into real crime. But Bill had insisted to everybody that they were just ordinary kids and they had come to fulfil the role he had prescribed for them. Both Bill and Lillian were delighted at their success. So were the villagers and farmers round about.

In due course Bill received his call-up papers. At his

preliminary interview he mentioned that he was a pacifist and as a result was sent to work in the Fire Service in Plymouth. After some months, however, he had to leave because of bad health. During the days at the cottage Bill and Lillian had become close friends of Frank and Mary Harris who taught at A. S. Neill's school, Summerhill, which was then evacuated to North Wales. They discussed schools and education and all that was wrong in that field until far into the night.

Frank and Mary had become regular visitors to the cottage during their school holidays and were deeply impressed by what they saw happening to Billy and Tom and were convinced that Bill and Lillian had a real flair for that kind of work. "Why don't you come up and see Neill?" asked Frank. "He'll probably give you a job in the school and you'll be doing the kind of work you're really interested in." It seemed obvious that they should give Summerhill a try although the last thing on earth Bill could imagine himself as at the time was a schoolteacher. Still, perhaps it would be different in a school, which according to Frank and Mary's description, embodied a revolutionary protest against everything he had formerly hated in the idea of school.

At the beginning of the following term Bill and Lillian joined the staff of Summerhill, Bill to teach History and Geography and Lillian to be housemother to the 'gangsters' —a dormitory of wild eleven-year-olds. As time went by Bill began to doubt his own ability as a teacher but saw that Lillian was having a tremendous success with her kids. Summerhill was making an enormous impact on him. He saw for the first time in his life children taking a real interest in a variety of subjects. He saw group discussion being held on a variety of political and cultural subjects and children saying what they really thought and taking part fearlessly. He saw them holding their own meetings to organize their own government. Here was the kind of pattern of education he was really looking for, one that would turn out intelligent, vital citizens.

In 1942 the post of warden of a small hostel for evacuee children in Bryn Conway became vacant and was advertised. Bill believed that it would suit him better than teaching and was confident that with Lillian as matron they could make a good job of it. He felt sure that somehow they had a combination of just the right personal qualities for it. Billy and Tom had taught them that. Neill had given them revolutionary ideas about how a community should really be run. They were both anxious to experiment on their own account and the problems of working-class children had a special attraction for them with their socialist outlook.

The hostel was bleak and cold when they arrived late in the afternoon on a bitterly cold day in January. For some time Bill just watched the dispirited-looking children mooching around when they arrived back from school each afternoon. Every now and then he heard himself being referred to as 'the man.' After his experience at Neill's school he felt himself protected against any impulse on his own part to make a sudden dramatic intrusion into their lives. He just left them for a bit, waited for them to make the first move and ask for something or at least exhibit some sort of reaction.

An unfinished scrap of his own account of his first experiences there perhaps gives the clue to his success: "After our first week there I put some sketches I had drawn on the walls of the playroom to brighten things up a bit. A few hours later they were on the floor. I asked a bunch of innocent-looking kids, who were drawing faces on the windows with their grubby fingertips, who had pulled down my pictures, and receiving no reply I allowed my voice to rise five or six octaves. 'Who the bloody hell pulled down my pictures?' I roared. The effect was electric. They all shot round, eyes wide open with mingled fright and astonishment. 'Ooh, he swore,' said one in amazement. 'Well, you swear, don't you?' I said. 'Oh no, sir,' he replied, 'and it was 'im who took down yer pitchers,' pointing to a hefty lout who scowled at me defiantly. 'So you did it. . . .' "

Bill's own story breaks off at this point. He does not recall exactly how he faced this tough ring leader who knew that normally he could mobilize all the other kids in the hostel behind him. He remembers only that he went straight into action before the boy had had a split second to glance round at his 'mates'. His 'training' in the Sydney Sailors' Home stood him in good stead. The boy was confronted with a kind of personality he had never faced before in such circumstances. The confrontation soon fizzled out. Without any actual physical violence Bill had won the first round.

This illustrates one of the fundamental paradoxes of Bill's approach. He believes in leaving individual children free, free often to do quite anti-social things, while they are really working out their problems but as soon as he scents a 'gang' reaction or detects the tones of a boy 'Hitler', he prepares himself to react with equal strength. He believes that this is the point where many with honest and genuine principles fall down in their work with difficult children. Sometimes because of their own personal weakness, sometimes in their attempt to be consistent in the application of their principles, they treat the gang leaders too gently and are overwhelmed by them, or at least lose their general sense of command. Sometimes they feel compelled to bring in outside force, probably the police. They thus fail in their object because unfortunately these children need protecting not exactly from the police but from that in themselves which would make them victims of the police. Unless either they or the police can understand this and allow for it they are almost bound to become life-long criminals.

After this first incident Bill let the days and weeks go by without making endeavours to do much and even the kids began to feel that more should be done to organize the place. They talked to him and he had his replies ready. He mentioned some of the ideas he had gathered from Neill's school, self-government in particular; though he had a strong inkling that he'd have to work out some modifications to suit these kids. At any rate he nonchalantly mentioned that he was prepared to help them in trying to organize themselves if they wanted it. And they did want it. They wanted it desperately, and all the security that went with it.

19

Meetings started but of course they didn't go smoothly at first. The kids had to learn to talk in order. One or two couldn't stand it when the feeling of the meeting went against them and on such occasions they would rush out kicking their chairs across the room and snarling 'bloody bastards' at everybody. This of course didn't disturb Bill. It gave him the opportunity to explain that in Australia the same expression is commonly used as a term of affection among the sheep hands on the stations. He thereby eliminated the element of morality in his own response, and in that of the children who remained with him, towards what would otherwise have been a socially unacceptable expression and an excuse for 'war'.

What it seems to me that Bill understood in these situations was that control over people and power to give orders are not, as is often supposed, one and the same thing. After his first encounter with the leader of that group of children in the hostel, Bill had control over the group but could not have given a single order. If he had given them an order he would have lost control over them. This is something that has to be learnt out under hard conditions with tough men. It was a thing that was to play a big part in his later successes with far tougher children in very much more difficult circumstances.

Little by little the meetings took real shape. I believe that they did so because Bill realized that he was facing a very different kind of situation from that which faced Neill at Summerhill. The kids there had a more secure, more cultured background. They were on the whole settled enough to see and want the advantages of self-government. Bill had to give a good deal of thought to how the meetings in this new human setting were going to work out. He saw two main kinds of danger, a Scylla and Charybdis which had to be skilfully steered through. On the one side there was the danger that the adults organizing things would use self-government as a subtle way of putting across their own rules and laws, in which case it would simply be an instrument to blunt the emotional reaction against authority in those taking part. It would be a kind of fraud. On the other side there was the danger that if the children were just left to run the thing for themselves, either the gang leaders would use the meetings to gain their own ends, or more probably the meetings would end up in futile chaos. No one would be carried a step further forward.

In the course of avoiding these twin dangers it seems to me that Bill evolved his own particular version of self-government meetings. He decided at the outset that he would get a firm grip on the meeting itself. He took the chair. He laid down a few simple rules for its orderly conduct: talking in turn only, accepting the vote of the majority. He made it quite clear that he intended to impose this basic order by any mental or physical means he thought necessary. He intended to quell any trace of 'gang' rebellion or any attempt by individual children to gain power. Having this control and order, however, he considered himself to be in a good position to allow the thoughts and feelings of individual children to be given a good hearing, so that they might feel that it really was they themselves who were beginning to form the laws and shape the social climate of the school or hostel. He intended that once a sufficient nucleus of the children had developed a great enough sense of responsibility towards the hostel, he would hand over the chairmanship to one of them.

Some fragments of a later meeting remain among the various records of progress at the hostel. A visitor was going to the hostel and met a small girl at the entrance. " 'That's our hostel, Bryn Conway.' 'Oh, I see you are evacuees. Where did you come from?' 'Liverpool,' she replied. 'How long have you been here?' 'Three years,' she replied with a slight sigh. 'Why don't you like being here?' I enquired. 'Well, I didn't like it much in the beginning, but it's different now and I don't mind being away from home as much as I did before. You see we have self-government and we always have something to do.' 'What do you mean by self-government?' I asked. 'Isn't there a warden and a matron in your hostel?' 'Oh yes, but they have to obey the laws we make, just like we do.' 'Laws,' I said, 'who makes the laws?' The girl looked a little sorry for me. 'We all do,

21

at the meeting. We have the meeting every week.' 'But supposing anyone breaks the laws,' I asked, 'are they punished or caned?' 'Certainly not! Bill, that is Mr. Malcolm (he likes us to call him Bill), said that if he or matron beat anyone that would be dictatorship, because if he did anything wrong we couldn't beat him because we're not strong enough and there'd be no need for laws. So you see . . .'

"Meanwhile Brian, who by this time was the regular chairman of the meeting (he's now the manager of a chain of restaurants in London) arrived on the scene and the conversation continued with him. 'What about your food and clothes, cleanliness and general health. Surely matron takes care of that?' 'Well,' he said slowly, 'matron has more chance to get to know about these things than we do, but at the general meeting all these things are brought up on the agenda. For instance, if we think that the meals are a bit dull we suggest changes. The cook attends the meetings and if possible the meals are made more interesting for us. Kids can be charged for using one another's towels or face cloths, and stuffing up the lav with paper which could cause disease. Bullying is not good for the kid who is being bullied or the bullier, so we have a very severe law against it. If anyone is found guilty of it the sentence is one week's early bedtimes and miss their cinema once. The road law is very severe too. If kids play in, or run into the middle of the road they may cause an accident and hurt someone else as well as themselves.'

"'But don't all these laws stop your fun?' I interrupted. Brian smiled, 'Oh no, we don't worry about the laws until we break them, and they are always being broken. But we do know why we shouldn't do these things and we do get a chance to say what really happened and defend ourselves. Before we had self-government I was often blamed for something I didn't do, and I bet others were too. It used to make me feel rotten and helpless.' Some of Brian's companions who had gathered round nodded vigorously and evidently with deep feeling.

" 'But who decides that a law shall be carried out?' I asked. 'Surely a committee can dictate to the rest just as much as one person can?' 'But we don't have a committee,' Brian replied, 'the members would get too uppish and bossy. I am the secretary of the hostel and often I am chairman of the meetings. All the charges are reported to me, and all the proposals for the weekly agenda, and I type them out. But everything is decided by majority vote. I can be charged by the smallest kid here. I am treated no better than anybody else, except that I go into Bill's room to type out the agenda, etc.' At that moment the lunch bell went and I arranged to visit the meeting after tea.

"When I arrived to pay my visit a few isolated scuffles were going on in the room. As I sat down with Bill, Brian shouted from the chair: 'Ready now. No noise. Anyone who interrupts or speaks out of turn will be charged. The first case for the tribunals this evening is Robert L, charged with bullying; witness: Willie H. Well Willie?' A wiry intelligent-looking boy of about eight years old stood up and said, 'Well, I saw Robert hit Jimmy G 'cross 'is face an' I charged 'im 'cos Robert is big.' Another boy, tall and well built, got up: 'I was making hats for the play,' he said, 'and Jimmy G kept snatching the scissors and cardboard all the time. I told him I would charge him for being anti-social and he said, "don't care," and kept on pestering me so I banged him.' 'Any other witnesses,' enquired Brian, looking around. 'Yes, I was,' said Bill, 'it happened exactly as Robert described it.' 'Well, Jimmy, what have you to say?' asked Brian. 'Robert L thinks he's everybody. I just wanted to borrow the scissors, an' they're not his anyway, and I think he's a bloody bully. So there!' Jimmy rattled this off without taking breath and glared belligerently round at everybody.

"Brian considered a while and then said slowly, 'Well, Robert's admitted that he hit Jimmy but it seems that Jimmy was as much to blame as Robert. The point is that Robert hit Jimmy and that is against self-government law, so I shall ask the meeting what is to be done in this case.' A thin fair girl raised her hand. 'Yes, Julie,' enquired Brian.

'I think this charge should be dismissed,' said Julie, 'but with a warning to both. Jimmy should not make such a nuisance of himself and Robert should not hit him.' Another girl put up her hand. Brian nodded. 'I agree with Julie's suggestion,' she said. 'Next time Jimmy annoys Robert, Robert should charge him and not take the law into his own hands. But Jimmy will have to be charged with being anti-social if he keeps on pestering the big ones.' 'Right,' said Brian, 'we'll have a vote on it. All those in favour of dismissing this charge, raise their hands.'

" 'Charge dismissed with a warning to both,' announced Brian and added, 'the rest of the charges I have here are for Sunday tribunals, so we shall carry on with the agenda. The first item on the agenda is "school" and Kitty wants to bring that up. Well, Kitty?' 'I want to know if anything can be done about our teacher. She hits us at the slightest excuse and makes favourites. At one of our meetings we decided to do nothing to annoy her because she seems to like hitting us and we have done our best not to annoy her. I don't think she likes us having self-government here but she shouldn't take it out on us.' Bill explained that he couldn't interfere in school matters. All he could do was to report it. 'But what about us? Surely something can be done?'

"Bill raised his hand. 'Yes, Bill,' said Brian. 'I'm sorry, Kitty, that I seem so feeble but I really cannot interfere in school matters. I do complain about it again and again but you see to some people our idea of self-government is new. The teacher's way of managing her class is accepted as normal by education authorities. As you all know I am hoping to obtain permission to run a school on self-government lines with teachers and housemothers sympathetic to our idea and resident in the school. This is the reason why I want to tell you all to be so careful what you do in the school and out of it. I am hoping that you will prove to all concerned that you have good social sense and that you are capable of governing yourselves. We have overcome difficulties and we shall have to meet many more. It has been admitted by responsible people judging by results that our idea does work well but it will take some time to convince the authorities that the type of school we have in view is needed in certain cases.'

"The next item on the agenda was brought up. It was the 'kitty'. All money brought to the hostel was pooled and used for collective outings to the cinema, sweets and certain amounts for each child on shopping expeditions. Everybody, however, kept a sharp eye on financial affairs and participated in the budget discussions. In this way any kind of social distinction among the children, which might have grown up on account of the size of the sums of money sent to them, was strangled at birth."

The visitor mentioned to Bill afterwards that he had heard it said that children tend to be far more severe with one another than adults would be if they were in charge. Bill pointed out that this was only so when a bullying type of child got control of the group. The average child, and the intelligent child particularly, wanted an atmosphere of peace and reasonableness within which to develop its interests. These interests may involve some boisterousness at times but are not antisocial.

Quick, forceful restraint of the child with a power urge to get control of other children as a mob, the fascist power to stimulate masses, is a characteristic feature of the kind of self-government which Bill seeks to establish and has succeeded in establishing with almost streamlined success. It is a feature which gives positive meaning to all the other well-known aspects of self-government and self-regulation for children. Bill is convinced that this kind of forceful restraint is necessary to allow real self-government and real self-regulation to develop.

The situation can be admirably illustrated from William Golding's *Lord of the Flies*. Although fictional this story seems to show profound insight into the ways of children and the unsuspected violence which is hidden beneath the forms of civilization and its threats. A group of schoolboys is stranded on a desert island after their aircraft has crashed. There are two possible leaders. One is rather reasonable and decent in spite of a little superficial boyish harshness. The other, who is the prefect of a choir school, proves, after a few weeks of primitive life, to be an unashamed nazi. The boys showed quite remarkable democratic tendencies on first landing and meeting together in a group. They chose their leader by a show of hands. The choir school prefect was rejected and he took his own class off as hunters for the party, chasing wild pigs for them to feed on. Finally he began to follow and kill those who disobeyed him, chasing them with the hunting cry, 'Kill the pig'. This death hunt became an intense mob urge.

Some critics have said that the story illustrates how a group of schoolboys can regress to conditions of savagery when the restraints of civilization are taken away. I believe that the story is only really understood if one sees how nearly the best lessons of civilization triumphed even in such a primitive situation. It occurred to me after I had watched the film of this story how excellently that little society of boys might have developed if there had been just one adult there to confront the little nazi leader right at the start, if there had been someone with superior physical strength who could have knocked him flat on the ground and then retired to some secret hideout, leaving the boys to work out their own problems and only existing as a threat to any possible development of mob violence.

This is all very hypothetical, of course, and yet is it not exactly what Bill was trying to do with his group of difficult children? It seems to me that this illustration helps to explain his paradoxical approach. For, on the one hand, he is always preaching that children should be left alone, free to develop in their own way. On the other hand, he has to excuse himself for acting in a way that must appear to contradict his own principles and taking what looks like very high-handed action indeed. To him it appeared as the only way to steer between those twin dangers of either using the meeting as a way of disciplining and ordering the children along conventional lines, or alternatively, allowing mob elements to stamp it out of existence or at least render it ineffectual. It seems to me that this explains how the tremendous sense of control, which Bill undoubtedly has over the children's meetings, is compatible with an equally evident sense that the children are developing in their own individual ways and in fact are doing all the real organizing in the community. As must have appeared from Brian's comments to the visitor, staff such as the matron for example were there as experts whose opinions were respected and upon whom the children would call for advice.

Many schools of the progressive and special kinds, of course, have meetings of a self-governing nature, but I know none in which the actual content of the discussion springs from, and so decisively creates the pattern of hostel or school life. Often meetings serve as very effective outlets or at least create a sense in those participating that their case is being heard. This helps to contain rebellious feelings rather in the traditional Hyde Park style, but it is something of a confidence trick and I believe that it is on those grounds that some heads of experimental schools, such as Mr. Lyward, reject the idea of self-government meetings. The meetings certainly do not appear to run in this way in the hostels and schools of which Bill has been in charge. The children have a far from illusory grasp on the running of things and one of the most noteworthy side effects of this is a remarkable increase in articulateness and readiness to speak up for themselves even among children of very poor backgrounds. Whereas in most state schools a bad social start leads to a progressive deterioration in actual educational attainment, in hostels and schools run by the Malcolms the community life seems to provide something that can go a long way towards overcoming the initial social handicaps. The success of the meetings run by the Malcolms was quickly recognized by the Caernarvonshire authorities. The Medical Officer for the County was from the beginning a staunch supporter of the Malcolms' and their self-government methods. The following letter illustrates this keen interest and shows that a great deal of additional interest was being aroused at the welfare department of the Ministry of Health:

"I have, as a matter of fact, in my subsequent travels about the country, told a good many people about the self-government meeting which I attended, about the excellent way in which the Chairman conducted the business and the part played by all persons present and I think it has excited a good deal of interest.

G. M. Aves, Chief Welfare Officer, Ministry of Health."

A brief account of the children at the hostel was compiled by the Medical Officer of Health, Dr. D. E. Parry-Pritchard. I believe that the full list must be quoted in order to give a sufficiently broad picture of what happened to a group of children who passed through the hostel. A number of the individual cases will be taken up later and considered more fully. (See pages 30, 31, 32.)

Such a report requires little interpretation but it may well arouse interest in a fuller knowledge of such children. The home backgrounds of Willy and Sally (included in this report), are outlined in a rather startling report made by the Liverpool and District Pacifist Service Unit. This report tells of the situation of the parents first: a mother who was something of an 'actress' and hated her husband who forgave her when she returned regularly to him after a series of affairs. This mother accused her husband of keeping mistresses and of other imaginary crimes and brought him twice to court, "once giving evidence that he was working while on unemployment benefit, and once giving evidence that he had stolen lead from his place of work; on the first occasion he went to prison." A sister of Sally and Willie, aged sixteen, had contracted V.D. and was living with a coloured sailor. "When the Unit first met the family, Willie was living with the rest of the family, except the father from whom his mother was separated. He was sleeping on a pile of urine-sodden rags with the rest of the children, on the bedroom floor. He was extremely dirty, hair long and matted. He was obviously undernourished though not underfed. It is believed that he had had only a few days' schooling, and no attempt was being made to send him to school. Like all the rest he had scabies, and his mother would not take them for treatment. He had no proper hygienic training and the lavatory in the yard was out of order.

"His mode of life was as Sally's companion, and the two of them were out in the streets whenever they could get away. They had been more than once warned by the police for stealing from bombed houses—what they stole they sold to second hand dealers, and bought chips, sweets and lemonade with the proceeds. Willie was an adept at earning pennies by asking for a penny for two ha'pennies and is reputed to have earned ninepence in a day by this means. He had a passion for destruction and his mother admitted that he had caused serious damage in two empty houses nearby, removing plumbing, woodwork and even brickwork. A good deal of damage in their own house, such as broken windows, was attributed to him. His mother accused him of the responsibility for many things of which he was no doubt innocent, and was completely unable to control him. ... He thought it quite normal to lie and honesty had to be presented to him as a new idea." The report goes on to say about all the children in the family: "They hated school, mainly because they were sent so irregularly and so dirty that they were always in trouble with the teachers. All used to wet the bed regularly and this seemed to be a symptom of anxiety as well as of bad training. All of them lied habitually since it was necessary to do so in self-defence and they were certain to receive unfair treatment if they told the truth. All of them stole, Sally with some accomplishment. Their whole attitude was one of rebellion and aggressive self-defence. They seemed to trust no one and to disobey or do wrong deliberately."

The authorities had commented that the cold atmosphere of the hostel had changed almost immediately on the arrival of the Malcolms. How much such children as Willie and Sally changed will be evident later from the reports they brought back to the hostel from the local council schools which they attended. Their performance varied in different subjects, of course, but conduct was invariably marked 'Good' or 'Very Good'.

Sex	Date Admitted	Age on Admission	Reason for Admittance	Date of Discharge	Progress when last Contacted
M	28/2/42	11	Beyond Control	9/5/46	Employed in Social Work with children. (1951)
M	4/3/42	9	Beyond Control	9/5/46	Employed in Factory. Amateur Boxing Champion. (1951)
M	10/8/44	11	Beyond Control	20/12/45	Employed as Gardener. (1947)
M	9/6/43	12	Nervous Instability	6/12/45	Employed in Social Work with children. (1951)
M	10/5/44	11	Delinquent	17/5/46	Was employed in firm of Commercial Artists. (1948)
M	27/10/44	13	Admitted temporarily whilst waiting vacancy in Approved School	10/1/45	Behaviour was good in Hostel, but as Court Order was made before admittance he passed onto Approved School when vacancy occurred.
M	10/10/44	12	Beyond Control	20/12/45	Pupil at Secondary School when last contacted. (1946)
F	24/8/44	14	Beyond Control	20/12/45	Employed in Laundry. (1947)
M	27/10/45	13	Absconding. Beyond Control	31/5/46	Responded to Hostel environment and returned home. (1946)
F	13/4/45	10	Beyond Control	7/8/45	Settled happily in Hostel. Transferred to London Residential School. (1945)
M	2/5/44	12	Nervous Instability	8/5/46	Taking final examination in Electrical Engineering. (1951)
F	10/8/44	12	Nervous Instability	20/12/45	Clerk in Offices of National children's organization. (1951)
M	5/7/44	11	Absconding. Beyond Control	10/8/46	Progress very satisfactory whilst at Hostel. Returned home. (1946)

M	8/5/44	6½	Beyond Control	20/9/46	Responded extremely well to Hostel environment. Returned home. (1946)
M	27/10/44	11	Admitted temporarily whilst waiting vacancy in Approved School	10/1/45	Responded very well to Hostel environment, but as Court Order was made before boy was admitted he was obliged to pass on to Approved School.
M	8/9/45	6½	Beyond Control	8/9/46	Headteacher reports: Getting on well with school work. Behaviour much improved. (1947)
M	22/10/45	10	Delinquent	9/5/46	Improved behaviour in Hostel and was considered a bright pupil at school. Absconded from Hostel after Malcolms left and returned home.
F	17/12/45	11	Incontinence of Urine. Difficult behaviour	11/11/46	Incontinence cleared up. Foster mother most pleased with her (1947)
M	9/10/44	12	Delinquent	6/12/45	Responded extremely well to environment in Hostel. Returned home (1945)
M	7/12/44	11	Bad home conditions. Truanting	3/7/46	M.O.H. and P.S.W. reported "acquired more social capacity, and quite well behaved". Conduct deteriorated after Malcolms left; Absconded, sent to Approved School.
F	9/3/45	10	Incontinence of faeces	11/7/45	Returned to London 1945. Incontinence still evident.

Sex	Date Admitted	Age on Admittance	Reason for Admittance	Date of Discharge	Progress when last Contacted
M	9/10/45	6¼	Incontinence. Delinquent	30/6/47	Boarded out when Hostel closed. Attended clinic but did not respond to treatment. Sent Approved School. (1947)
M	14/5/45	11	Incontinence of faeces. Truanting	14/5/46	Incontinence cleared up. "General progress very satisfactory." (1950)
F	9/2/46	10	Peculiar noises in throat. Fainting bouts	25/8/46	Settled down well in Hostel, but epileptic condition became worse. Transferred to Epileptic school. (1948)
M	31/3/44	10	Delinquent	17/5/46	Responded well to Hostel environment. Returned home. (1946)
F	10/8/44	8	Beyond Control	20/12/45	Responded well to Hostel environment. Returned home. (1945)
M	10/8/44	6	Beyond Control. Incontinence of faeces	20/12/45	Incontinence cleared up. Returned home. (1945)
M	10/8/44	10	Beyond Control	20/12/45	Responded well to Hostel environment. Returned home. (1945)
M	31/3/44	10	Incontinence of Urine. Beyond Control	17/5/46	Incontinence cleared up. Returned home. Pupil at Secondary school. (1947)
F	1/5/43	11	Beyond Control	1/5/46	Set up own Hairdressing business. (1951)
M	21/4/43	9	Incontinence of Urine. Beyond Control	10/9/45	Incontinence cleared up. Returned home. (1945)

2

Experience in War-time
Evacuation Hostels

As a result of their success at the little hostel at Bryn Conway, the Malcolms were asked to take over the Regional Evacuation Hostel at Penybrin, where the most difficult children from the counties of North Wales were sent. They had been warned before going there that there was a cold atmosphere in the hostel itself and that local people were constantly complaining about acts of theft and vandalism committed by the children of the hostel. The nucleus of responsibly minded children, which had formed at Bryn Conway, accompanied Bill and Lillian to the new hostel. The task of dealing with this fresh group of children was thus made much easier since they could witness other children from the same sort of backgrounds as themselves acting reasonably and without any resentment against what they assumed to be the 'authorities'.

His experiences with even such a small group as he had had at Bryn Conway convinced Bill that the whole system for dealing with young offenders was harsh and wrong. It just did not take into account some of the children's backgrounds nor did it seem to have any machinery for giving such children a good new start. They were really very easy to turn into responsible children in nearly all cases. It just seemed that somehow they had got themselves caught in a vicious circle of reaction against authority. The more authority tried to do against them the more they stepped up their retaliation and by this process they were being driven into becoming full-blown criminals.

B

With a small but obviously fairly representative group of children Bill had stopped this process. He believed that he did it partly by merely being what he was. He was not a schoolmaster. He was not the authoritarian type. But he did believe that people should be free to regulate themselves and he was prepared to take action, very positive action, against children or adults who tried to stop this happening. He felt confident that he was simply adapting the ideas on education which he had found at Summerhill to the special needs of deprived and homeless working class children.

His fight in this cause led to one harsh encounter with the operation of official justice, one which I think reveals the strength, and indeed the bitterness of his feelings on this subject. A small boy of thirteen, accompanied by police constables and the following court order to Bill, arrived at the hostel:

IN THE COUNTY OF CAERNARVON

Petty Sessional Division of Caernarvon

TO each and all of the Constables of the County of Caernarvon and to the Occupier of the Place of Safety at the North Wales Regional Evacuation Hostel, Penybrin, in the parish of Llanbelig, in the said County.

BEFORE the Juvenile Court sitting at the County Hall, Caernarvon, in the said County Alan Wynne Jones of Caerwen Fawr, Cilgwyn, Carmel, a child, having been ordered by the juvenile court sitting in the County Hall aforesaid, this day, to be sent to an Approved School, and the operation of the committal Order being postponed:

IT IS ORDERED that the said Alan Wynne Jones be taken to the Occupier of the Place of Safety at the North Wales Regional Evacuation Hostel, Penybrin, in the parish of Llanbelig in the said County, and be there detained until he is sent to an Approved School in pursuance of the Approved School Order, such detention not to exceed more than twenty-eight days from the date of this order, unless otherwise ordered.

YOU, the said Constables, are therefore commanded to convey the said Alan Wynne Jones to the said place of safety and there deliver him to the person in charge thereof, together with this warrant; and you, the Occupier of the said Place of Safety, to receive him into your custody and detain him as aforesaid.

The language alone made Bill furious. It seemed to him

inhuman in a way that words could scarcely express. They could deal in houses in this fashion if they liked but children 'no!' Of course he received Alan into his custody and detained him as aforesaid. A short while later he did the same for the boy's younger brother Selwyn but not without a number of fiery letters passing backwards and forwards between himself and the Clerk to the Justices.

In December, after a couple of extensions of the boys' 'detention' had been granted, Bill received the following letter from the Clerk: "I have been informed today that the above named boy (Selwyn) can be admitted this month to the Bryn Estyn Approved School, Wrexham. I am to be informed later of the exact date of admission.

"I shall therefore be much obliged if you will be so kind as to let me have a full report on the conduct of the boy whilst he has been at your Home, at your earliest convenience."

To this Bill replied immediately as follows: "The above named boy was admitted to this Hostel on 27th October, 1944. Since that time he has displayed a modest, sensitive demeanour and has shown a pathetic eagerness to fit in with his surroundings.

"He attends the Central School in Caernarvon and I have not received any report of behaviour difficulties from his teachers.

"If my information is correct the boy has not been guilty of any serious delinquency. The unfortunate situation to which the child was reduced was very obviously a reaction to his home circumstances and environment.

"He is of normal intelligence but intensely shy and diffident, and this fact, I think, tends to create in the mind of the casual observer a false impression of his mental abilities.

"I am of the opinion that if the suggestion of removing the boy to an Approved School is carried out, the effect on the child will be disastrous."

In the meantime Bill had heard from the boys' mother that she wished to visit the Hostel and wrote her the following letter: "I have just received a communication from the Medical Officer of Health to the effect that if you or your husband wish to visit your children here, you must make application to him before doing so.

"Please address your letter to the Medical Officer of Health, County Offices, Caernarvon. (Bill knew there would be no opposition from that quarter.)

"The boys are settling down quite nicely, and I think they are fairly happy. They have plenty of diversions to occupy their minds and I think that they like their new school. With kind regards etc."

The use of the word 'disastrous' in Bill's previous letter to the Clerk of the Justices had caused some considerable stir. He received two replies: one from the Clerk and another from the Psychiatric Officer of the County: "Your letter of the 12th instant was submitted to a Juvenile Court here yesterday. You are doubtless aware that an Order has already been made for the sending of this boy to an Approved School.

"Adverting to the last paragraph in your letter, stating that the removal of the child to an Approved School would be 'disastrous', the Justices have asked me to request you to give your reasons for this statement.

"One of the Justices sitting yesterday, who has visited Bryn Estyn School, says that it affords a wonderful open-air life and that it gives opportunities for attending to bees, rabbits and poultry, learning joinery and other pursuits, and that every incentive is given to enable boys there to take up an ordinary life. In fact, it is a very happy secondary school.

"It is my intention, when sending your report to the school, to say that the Justices expressed a wish that the two brothers should not be separated. The Home Office have been informed of this and it is hoped that arrangements can soon be made to enable Alan Wynne Jones to join his brother."

A further letter arrived from the Psychiatric Officer of the Council, containing the paragraph: "The Assistant to the Clerk to the Justices has stated that your letter regarding the above named caused the Magistrates to make strong comment in as much as you would appear to criticise their decision and used the word 'disastrous'."

Bill reflected on the narrow shave Billy and Tom had had in Cornwall and felt mad at the implacability of the law even in its dealings with the young. It was not a matter of any personal criticism of anybody. It was just that he felt that he had really come to know the situation of the two brothers while they had been in the hostel. He felt convinced that underneath they were really sensitive and slightly weak children. He saw them as victims of a law which failed to discriminate and judged too much merely by outward behaviour. When he had calmed down he wrote his reply to the Clerk to the Justices: "My remarks relative to an Approved School for the above named child were not in any way intended to cast aspersions on any particular school. But I do think that it can be admitted that children do display a very evident fear when they are threatened with being sent to an Approved School.

"These unfortunate children do need special treatment to help them re-adjust themselves with ordinary society, and I feel that the orthodox methods of discipline would not be very helpful in this case, and to part the children, even for a short time, would alarm and upset Selwyn's brother who is not mentally strong. Both children seem to be happy and well and they are responding well to our methods of treatment. Naturally I am not anxious that the children should go at this stage of their improved development."

Both brothers, however, did go to the Approved School at the beginning of January, 1945, but that was not quite the end of the story. In the Summer of the same year a letter arrived from the boys' father who had just returned from fighting on the continent:

"Dear Matron and Mr. Malcolm,
Just a line or two on Behalf of Mrs Jones, and myself, a vote thank you very much for the welcome, and Kindness you gave my two Boys, Selwyn, Alan, who is at present at Bryn Estyn. I Did visit them four weeks ago, and first thing they Did Show me was many Letters from you Both. this is very nice of you, and best of luck to you in the Good work you Have Done, and still Keep Doing. I do Believe the Boys will remember you for Ever after the time they Have Been under your kind care first chance I will

get, I will be to Glad to come personol to see, you, Both on my next leave.

I am Glad of Been out for my Country, and fighting for Freedom of good Friends like you Both.

I Do Hope you will take my warmest vote of thanks for good work, and I am sure 'God will pay you' iff me and Mrs. Jones cant."

Perhaps there is a reflection here of that same 'pathetic eagerness' that Selwyn had shown in the Hostel. It was a clear case of well-intentioned and sincere working class parents unable to cope with the pressures of society and the strains of war through sheer lack of education and understanding of how things work. What fight could such a father have put up against the seemingly irrevocable decision of the magistrates? Had he been better educated he might have obtained compassionate leave and sought legal assistance to defend his sons.

It was with the cause of such people that Bill felt that he was identifying himself in his work. He felt it to be scandalous that while a father was away fighting for the freedom of his society, punitive measures should be taken against his children. He believed passionately that the least that society owed him was to try to understand and protect his children. He felt sure that however well-intentioned and sympathetic might be the work of Approved Schools, however successful they might be in reforming the wayward character, they left a stigma on the child who passed through them.

We know from recent research that the child tends to reinforce the judgments, and fulfil the prophesies made about him. We know this especially in the case of low streams in secondary schools in regard to academic attainment. We have good reason to suspect that the same may be true of behaviour 'streaming'. But even apart from how the child is affected by being faced with, and having been at an Approved School there can be little doubt that the average employer tends to attach considerable importance to a boy's record. The most recent Government publication on this subject, 'Statistics relating to approved schools, remand homes and attendance centres in England and Wales for the year 1962', does not present an encouraging picture of the ability of these institutions to reform. Back in 1945 Bill believed that he had seen enough of the effect of punitive institutions in the area where his family lived in Liverpool to be convinced himself about the environmental factors in the fostering of crime. He had seen it in Australia too.

Within the Hostel Bill observed with some satisfaction the development of a real self-governing community of boys and girls. As time went on he noted a steadily decreasing need for the meetings and the children's tribunals as the children's natural sense of self-regulation developed. They began to see for themselves the things that they couldn't do on account of living in a community. They began to see also that there were other things they couldn't do because of the wider society outside. They began to notice that some of these restrictions, which came from outside, were really necessary and others seemed only artificial. They became aware that they had to accept the standards of people outside, and respect them, if they were to keep the little community in which they lived free and intact. They had to accept school for instance. They had to accept the outside world's standards of behaviour when they were in it. They had to accept their parents' standards of behaviour when they were with them. They had learnt a freedom in the hostel which had enabled them to respect other people's views and freed them from the compulsion to react emotionally against them.

The love of camps and adventurous outdoor games, the freedom of dress, the absence of adult control often led the children at Penybrin to look very much like those stranded boys on their desert island in *Lord of the Flies*. On one or two occasions local inhabitants with prudish inclinations lodged complaints about almost naked children swinging like monkeys from the trees in the Hostel grounds. These complaints, however, were taken care of by the Medical Officer of Health for the County, upon whose protection Bill felt himself able to rely completely. Some official visitors were surprised at the almost total lack of supervision exercised over the children. But to Bill this was essential. They could not be 'free' *and* supervised.

In spite of the high handed action that had been necessary in the early stages of establishing the hostel, freedom and self-government really were the cardinal principles of its life. It was sometimes hard to make people see this. It still is, especially in educational circles. Despite all advances in this sphere, it is still very widely felt that the fundamental job of education is to instil attitudes of obedience. To be able to take orders with the right grace is widely regarded as the hallmark of a good and successful education. Neill and Homer Lane before him held to the revolutionary, though today thought to be somewhat discredited, verse of Shelley's:

> The man
> Of virtuous soul commands not nor obeys.
> Power like a desolating pestilence
> Pollutes whate'er it touches: and obedience,
> Bane of all genius, virtue, freedom, truth,
> Make slaves of men, and of the human frame
> A mechanized automaton.

It is very important to remember that Bill believed himself to be operating and developing entirely within this tradition. He would have no truck with developments in education which he thought were using the machinery of self-government to instil conventional attitudes of obedience. He was beginning to become fully aware, however, of some of the modifications which were necessary to adapt the ideas of free education to suit the needs of the kind of children who were sent to him.

The children he had been with at Summerhill had had on the whole wide, educated backgrounds even if they were usually unorthodox and unconventional. Like all young children they had, in many cases, been prone to interpret even the most unorthodox behaviour of the parents rather rigidly. Bill saw that they needed a release from their backgrounds, even needed opportunities for destruction. But they did have backgrounds and firm strong backgrounds at that. He found, on the other hand, that his children frequently had an awful emptiness in their backgrounds and had found only too many opportunities for destruction. They were background*less* in a stark and terrible sense. That seemed to be why they were so anxious to fit into school life and make a success of it. Even the order of daily attendance at school, when proceeded to from the free atmosphere of the Hostel, could give them something which they desperately needed. This was a discovery which was to have great importance later when Bill came to take charge of schools himself. Here in Penybrin the children were settling down excellently in the local schools: the Caernarvon Council Boys' School and the Central School. Bill had put their schooling in such perspective that they appeared to be gaining great strength from their success at it. In December 1944 Willie—mentioned in the previous chapter—brought back his report to Bill: Reading was Good, Writing and Composition Very Weak, Arithmetic only Fair but Drawing was Fairly Good. Geography and History were his star subjects and both were Good. He was proud to show it to Bill for in the section covering Conduct at the bottom it stated clearly in bold letters 'Very Good'. His position in his class was low but what an achievement it was both for Willie and for Bill when one considers the report on his background at the end of the previous chapter. The next year a similar report followed. Some improvement in his weak subjects was evident and his conduct was again 'Very Good'. Even the two boys who were sent on to Approved School had Very Good for Conduct on their reports while they were at Bill's hostel. Others also came back with very good reports, most with apparently good academic results although it is impossible to gauge the prevailing standards of the schools which were hit not only by evacuation problems but also by the severe staffing problems brought on by the war. Some teachers had added, 'A quiet sensible boy' or girl. Out of these children a few went on to Grammar Schools later and one succeeded in entering university.

The county had long been taking this kind of success for

granted. Of one boy the County Welfare Organizer wrote to Bill: "The teacher has complained that K has been taking food from his foster parents' store and when he was spoken to about it, he flew into a wild passion and threatened to run away. The teacher also complains that he lies and pilfers and that he encouraged three boys of nine to interfere with the public lavatories. He has a brother, Stephen, at the hostel at Criccieth but the Matron does not wish to have K as he has a very bad influence on his younger brother. I do not think you will have any bother with him. I expect it is just a question of management." In another letter the same person wrote to Bill; "I went to a meeting on juvenile delinquency at the Home Office last week. I could not help feeling that if Remand Homes and Approved Schools were run on self-government lines that many a young scamp would be saved from becoming an out and out criminal at a later date." And then later in the same letter she went on to refer to the headmistress of a local school: "I wish you and Mrs. Malcolm would ask her to supper, not once but many times until she becomes imbued with your spirit, discuss the children and your treatment of them with her in a friendly way, ask her to make an effort to attend your meetings. She cannot fail to be impressed and after a little while she may adopt your methods herself . . . In this way you may even get Self-government in school which would be ideal."

There were many problems still in the future. The children in the hostel, being evacuated, had to make the hostel their full-time home. Little contact was made with the parents as they were usually far away and engaged on war work. Only the weekly letter, which most of them asked Lillian to have a look at before posting, maintained continuity in this respect and gave Bill and Lillian an idea of how things were going in that quarter. Relations between schools the Malcolms were later to run and parents were obviously going to be much more complicated and delicate than they were in the Hostel, tucked away as it was in a remote corner of Wales.

At the end of the war when the Hostel was about to close down Bill wrote his own comments on their work and outlined the kind of education his experience with evacuee children had shown would be necessary for dealing with the broad problems of delinquency and maladjustment, which were obviously on the horizon:

"During the war years the problem of Juvenile Delinquency has become extremely acute and it is evident that, if the unfortunate children involved are not to become a future liability to the nation, something must be done to help them now. There are of course a number of local authorities who are doing all they can to help the children under their care, in the face of great difficulty, and the Government has recently set up a committee of enquiry which will inevitably bring to light some of the causes of this social evil. In the meantime, however, it would be as well to encourage experiment in the existing Children's Homes, Hostels, Remand Homes and Approved Schools, the results of which could be examined for a subsequent scientific approach to the solving of the problem.

"Through the upheavals of war etc. . . . Obviously the difficulties of the children have their roots in their formative years either because of the conditions of wretched poverty (of spirit as well as body) in which they lived or, if they come from higher social strata, because of broken homes and consequent insecurity. To punish such children for delinquencies engendered by the influences of their environment is, to say the least, short-sighted . . . The Borstal and Approved School systems have not been very successful in dealing with the problem and their failure is mainly due, I believe, to the policy of sex segregation carried out in these institutions. To separate a hundred or so adolescent boys away from all feminine society for years at a time is simply asking for perversion, and their attitude to feminine company when they leave their place of detention could not be expected to be normal, and so their difficulties begin all over again. The need for experiment is obvious and I feel, from our experience, that a school for delinquents of average intelligence and run on co-educational lines would point the way to the solving of a very difficult problem.

"We cannot expect children brought up in the slums of the great cities to become socially conscious citizens when they are given absolutely no real training in citizenship. . . ."

Bill's report goes on to advocate more concentration of attention and resources on the children of between six and twelve years of age and then outlines the work at Penybrin:

"At the beginning of 1943 we began an experiment in self-government at this hostel for difficult evacuee children (thirty boys and girls with an age range from six to fourteen). The majority were handicapped by their inability to adjust themselves socially, but amongst them were a few suffering from much more serious disturbances. After the first six weeks we discovered, in the case of the former, that the environment of what we have called 'ordered freedom' was enough in itself to give the children a focus point and they improved both physically and mentally. They ceased their anxious feeling and plucking at our clothes and their almost hysterical desire to be petted and kissed. They were finding their security in the certainty of approval and a just environment. They began to develop a sturdy independence and various officials, who visited the hostel, were very much impressed by the way they conducted their General Meetings and Children's Tribunals. We had our bad periods but these were clearly due to circumstances outside our control. One local schoolteacher seemed to take pleasure in dealing out indiscriminate punishment and for days afterwards the children would let out their hate and frustration in the hostel. The relationship between the school and the hostel run on these lines is always liable to be difficult. If the children are fortunate enough to have interested and sympathetic teachers as our children did at the Central School here, then they really like going to school, and our work is not constantly being frustrated. But the relationship cannot always be so fortunate and that is my strongest reason for suggesting setting up a co-educational self-governing school as an experiment that might point the way to solving the oncoming problems of delinquency. . . .

"It would be a mistake for me to suggest that I think that

all the problems of childhood can be cured by the principles set out above. They cannot effectively improve the child of *proved* subnormal intelligence but it must be remembered that he is rarely an active delinquent . . . I have noted that the method has been particularly successful with children who steal or are suffering from sexual maladjustment. Stealing is a symbolic act in these children in the majority of cases and when they actually feel secure they cease to steal. Sex is not treated as a guilty secret in our community and is discussed more or less openly *but not consciously or deliberately* and usually only when the children happen to bring it up. . . ."

In this report Bill emphasised the need for dealing with difficult children before it was too late; "It is fairly certain that without understanding guidance, the difficult child of from seven to twelve will develop into the delinquent of from twelve to sixteen and thence to the criminal of later years. The sensible course therefore is to spend more time, money and patience on the difficult child between seven and twelve." Failures he certainly had later both at Alresford and at Childscourt but most of them were among children forced on him by circumstances.

In reply to this report the Director of Education for the County commented; "I may, I hope, be allowed to say how convincing a case you establish for a more widely enlightened approach to the difficult social problem you are tackling . . . We shall recognize how dependent we are for a solution upon the pioneer experimental work you are carrying out." The comments of the Clerk to the Gwyrfai Rural District Council on the Malcolms' work is also interesting since it bears the imprint of genuine praise and is clearly not a piece of automatic and nominal testimony.

"This hostel was established under the Government Evacuation Scheme in order to provide accommodation for all the difficult children evacuated to the six North Wales Counties and during the whole of this period it has been administered by this Council.

"It was first established in 1940, and we had very great difficulty with some of these children. Several of them ran away and thefts from local shops were frequent, and there was always a cold atmosphere around this hostel, which was remarked upon by some of the chief officials of the Welsh Board of Health.

"In February 1944 Mr. and Mrs. Malcolm were appointed Warden and Matron and there was an immediate change in the whole atmosphere. The hostel became a happy home and we have had no trouble with any of the children. Some of the children were really bad characters but are now on the way to becoming useful citizens . . . The place is now a home in the real sense of the word, and it is significant that some of the children who have gone home still come back there for a short holiday."

At the beginning of 1945 an incident occurred which shocked the public's conscience. Two boys who had been boarded out under the Government's evacuation scheme suffered such severe ill-treatment that one of them subsequently died and the incident led to the setting up of a public enquiry by the Home Secretary. One well known Sunday newspaper using the public interest stirred up by the death of one of the O'Neill brothers ran an article on Bill's work:

"I have seen how one authority is tackling the problem of boys and girls with much the same background as the O'Neill brothers."

The writer concluded his article with one highly significant comment.

"The Warden has studied psychology and seasons it with much common sense."

(*Reynolds News*, 25.3.45.)

In 1946 the Hostel finally closed. Bill found himself out of work and in search of a job. The education authorities in North Wales showed much interest in his ideas and in the success of his work. But the problem as far as they were concerned had largely disappeared with the return of the evacuated children to their city homes. In any case they were far too busy implementing other more pressing requirements of the 1944 Act.

Bill eventually took charge of a hostel for delinquent boys in Essex. He remained there only for a short time but was confronted with one of the toughest individual problems which had ever faced him. One afternoon he received a telephone call from the local hospital. The Matron, who knew of his work, had contacted him because they had a boy in the hospital who had attacked a couple of nurses with a large carving knife and had threatened to 'get' the Matron herself and one of the doctors. He was locked up in one of the wards and it was desperately urgent that someone should do something for him immediately. Bill agreed to go at once. When he entered the ward he found the boy standing on a table. He went straight up to him leaving the door open behind him and suggested he should "come and try our place". The following is an account written by one of the welfare workers concerned at the time: "An example of these methods in an individual case is Dennis. He was an uncouth lad hating everything and everybody. His resentful acts of aggression had met with severe punishment from early childhood. Arriving at the hostel he suddenly grunted savagely, rushed into the dining room and put his hand through half a dozen windows. He took the fireguard from the grate and jumped on it until it was completely flat. Similar outbursts of unrestrained behaviour continued for a period. Mr. Malcolm persevered in his attempts to gain the boy's trust, using no sanction against him except to remark casually that it was very cold with the windows out, and waited patiently for a sign of response to come from the boy.

"On a later occasion Dennis went out all day. When he returned Mr. Malcolm asked him quite pleasantly if he had had a good time. Dennis snarled, rushed into his room and put his fist through another pane of glass. This time he cut himself, and after looking at the cut in horror, he reluctantly approached Mr. Malcolm to show him. Mr. Malcolm made quite a job of binding it up and also put his arm in a huge sling, hoping that Dennis might unbend in the process. Dennis, however, merely grinned defiantly and walked off without a word. He kept the sling on for a few weeks after the cut had healed. For about five months Dennis remained absolutely unapproachable, until one night his housemother complained that he had got into bed with his clothes on.

About half an hour later terrific roars were heard coming from his bedroom. Mr. Malcolm dashed in thinking that Dennis was attacking someone. In actual fact he was calling 'Bill,' as Mr. Malcolm was known to the children.

"When he arrived in the room Dennis was lying in bed with the clothes drawn up to his eyes. By the side of his bed was a heap of wool which had once been a jersey, picked into very small pieces. He had also cut his pyjamas into very small pieces with a pair of scissors. The bed was in a filthy state with mud off his boots and covered with his own excrement. It was almost the lad's final act of aggressive resentment against a world which he felt did not want him. Mr. Malcolm sensed this and remarked, 'Well, son, I bet it took you quite a while to make this mess, and I expect you feel quite satisfied. Now I will just clean all this up and get you some clean sheets—you mucky so-and-so!' He then obtained some clean sheets from the airing cupboard, made Dennis comfortable and cleared up the mess round the bed. As he was turning away he said goodnight to Dennis who gazed up at him and murmured, 'You silly old sod,' but with a humorous twinkle in his eye which converted this phrase to a term of affection. This was the first time the child had shown any human feeling apart from hate."

Such was the story of Dennis. His further recovery was a matter of time. I found it remarkable how Bill managed to contain such a violent character within a community of very much more normal children but I recently commented to him that his treatment of Dennis seemed particularly gentle in comparison with his handling of the first group of children in Bryn Conway. "It had to be gentle," he replied, "he was like a ferocious animal. You couldn't kick him in the teeth any more than you could a tiger!"

It was clear that Dennis was amongst those with whom Bill had dealt, who really did need some kind of special treatment. He was in a worse condition than any of the children in the Hostel. But even there it should be recalled there were a "few who were suffering from much more serious disturbances" according to Bill's report quoted earlier. He was coming to believe that this small percentage might need some kind of treatment, but that the other much larger percentage were included in the category of 'difficult', 'emotionally disturbed', 'maladjusted' or whatever it happens to be called, seemed to him to indicate something wrong with the social and educational environment from which they came and some fundamental fault in the methods of categorization. They were not abnormal children and if society couldn't contain them, then there was something wrong with society. Dennis and a few like him were different. It was almost impossible for any community to contain him and he really did need a very special approach.

The following year the Malcolms were to face a new challenge. Their success had been noted by various Local Authorities. They were asked to take over an establishment in Maidenhead for really tough delinquent boys. Experimental attempts by psychiatrists to deal with their aggression and violence had failed and they had become an extreme problem to the local police. They had become, to all appearances at least, an organized body of young criminals. One of them was later to become a notorious murderer. In what was now his characteristic fashion Bill brought order to this unruly mob of boys. Before long he had introduced them to the ways of self-government and they were able to go round Maidenhead as freely as respectable citizens.

News of the Malcolms' work and successes had reached the national newspapers and they had become known amongst groups of private people interested in the welfare of children and the post-war problems of delinquency. One such group of people had formed a committee with the intention of opening a school "to adjust socially maladjusted children" and was known as *Children's Social Adjustment Limited*. Two of its members visited Bill and Lillian at Maidenhead and discussed a project which seemed likely to open the way to developing almost at once the kind of school Bill had so long dreamed of, and which he had discussed so enthusiastically with those young evacuees in Wales.

3

The Malcolms at
Alresford Place School

In the Spring of 1948 Bill and Lillian moved into Alresford
Place in Hampshire to prepare for the opening of a new
school in the Autumn. It appeared as though at last they
were going to have the opportunity to experiment with their
ideas and to create a school close to their ideals. They were
going to have trained teachers, who were specialists in the
sort of problems they would have to face, and while the
actual job of teaching was to be in their hands, classroom
discipline, individual children's difficulties in concentration
and the overall arrangement of lessons were to come within
the sphere of the school meeting which Bill directed. He
decided that it should now be held every morning to cope
with the extra problems with which it was going to be
concerned and also to air everybody's grievances and so give
a good start to each day.

The prospect was good but the venture was doomed from
the start to fall short of all the ideals for which Bill had
striven. The seeds of what was to frustrate his work were
already evident in an article in the *Times Educational Supple-
ment*, published shortly after the school opened: "The work
of Alresford Place is under the supervision of a management
sub-committee of the Council of Management." There
was also an Advisory Committee composed of more members
than it was intended there should be children in the
school! The school was visited every fortnight by the
Honorary Psychiatrist who was also, for a great deal of the

time, chairman of the management committee. She was a spinster of nearly seventy years of age and held strong and somewhat unusual views on how the problems of disturbed children should be tackled. It was plain that the whole structure of the organization was top-heavy and that sooner or later it would bear down disastrously on an individualist like Bill who had his own distinctive ideas about how he would tackle the tasks ahead of him.

He very soon found that there was one important difference between the situation in which the children in Wales had found themselves and that in which the children at Alresford were placed. The children in Wales were free in the hostel, to which they were sent for their 'crimes', but they attended an ordinary school and they ended up with excellent leaving reports from an ordinary school. Their earlier records had very little bearing on their opportunities in later life and in most cases they found good jobs suited to their abilities. In fact their time at the hostel had plainly helped them to achieve the satisfactory positions in life which are listed in the report of the Caernarvon Health Department. Bill's main reason for opposing the sending of the Jones brothers to the Approved School was that he felt it would constitute ultimately a handicap to their achievement of a position in life suited to their abilities. Now he was beginning to feel that the children at Alresford Place, with all the emphasis which was being placed upon their being in the category of 'maladjusted' both by the education authorities and even more by the school's own committee, were going to find themselves with similar handicaps. He believed that this categorization would affect them both objectively and subjectively unless they made very rapid recoveries and did very well in a normal secondary school for some years before leaving. He considered it improbable that children who had been with him for a short time and then gone back to their old school and home situation would shine in school like the children in Wales. In any case he wanted his school to be a place for equipping the children who came to him for dealing with life in all its aspects.

It is of course possible to argue in two ways from the impressions which Bill reported. Either it would be better to go back to the hostel-plus-normal-school situation for disturbed children, or else it was essential to regard the school side of the 'special school' as being in all senses normal. Bill was determined to follow the latter course and to eradicate from the minds of the children, their parents and, if possible, any adults connected with them the least suspicion that there was anything abnormal about Alresford Place School. The repercussions from this, which will appear throughout the rest of the book, were tremendous and sometimes illogical. Many people who showed an interest in the work of the school were distinctly disturbed by Bill's attitude. Their *interest* lay in the fact that the school was something special, different. Some plainly liked to dramatize themselves as people with an interest in psychologically disturbed children. To Bill this categorization of children was one factor which was rapidly leading to a strong anti-psychiatric bias in his thinking. He felt that the psychiatrist tended to reinforce the child's sense of being in a special category.

The Chairman of the Committee, who was also the Honorary Psychiatrist, had previously worked with David Wills at 'Q' Camps. These camps, begun before the war, were for 'maladjusted youths' and were intentionally primitive, 'a group of simple huts in an Essex field'. She brought with her a mode of thinking about disturbed and deprived children which Bill was beginning to feel was the reverse of the conclusions he was drawing from his own experience. He was well aware of the value of camp and outdoor life for all children. But he was becoming increasingly convinced that the first and most essential thing for deprived children was a good, almost sumptuous environment; surroundings in fact which made them gasp for a moment or two on arrival. He did not, of course, believe that the effects of deprivation could be undone in a moment but he felt sure that 'rich' surroundings could be used as a means of aiming a shrewd blow at the child's own sense of deprivation. They could be the beginning of a child's rethinking over his lot in the world.

Bill believed also that really good surroundings are a deterrent to destructive urges which are encouraged by the sight of things which are poor, cheap, shoddy or already half-destroyed. The Committee plainly held the opposite belief. This received practical expression in the old second-hand iron bedsteads, the ex-N.A.A.F.I. tables and chairs and the other poor quality equipment which was supplied to the school. Bill was becoming increasingly sure that the children with him needed a warm, comfortable, secure centre from which they could face the problems of life afresh. Camps and the rough life were something for secure children. They could, and they did come later.

One of the most important questions to arise during the initial development of the new school was how the lessons were going to be organized. Were they to be voluntary or compulsory? Should an attempt be made to go back to the original concept of free education as it was practised at Summerhill? Was it the best thing for these particular children? Was the freedom which the children in Wales had sufficient to enable them to cope with a measure of compulsion? Might not some enforced schooling even be more appropriate for these children upon whom society had already placed such serious practical handicaps? Bill decided to resolve these problems by making the lessons voluntary at first and later bringing up the whole matter at the school meetings. It soon became obvious that a big special debate would have to be devoted to the subject. This was arranged and the children at Alresford Place discussed their own 'Education Bill'. The following are some extracts of accounts made by a teacher at the time:

"Speaker
(Bill):   We will debate once again whether we should have compulsory school and whether we should be kept quiet in class.
Kim: I suggest that we should have voluntary school and we have two days a week when we must go to school. We should have silence in class.

John:	I think school as it is now is all right and it would be better if we had the other lessons like gardening.
Linda:	I think it is all right as it is now. I think we should have free school but those who do not come to English and Arithmetic should miss Art.
Bob:	I disagree with that because if some of us are not interested in being a schoolteacher but rather in being an artist it is not fair to stop us going to the things which would be more useful to us.
John:	I agree with Bob. I don't think that if they do not go to Arithmetic they should miss other subjects. Some people don't like Arith. There should be compulsory school and people should be able to choose their own lessons.
Speaker:	I suggest that when children are in class they should have sanctions to keep them quiet.
John:	You already have one. When they make a noise you have been putting them to bed.
Speaker:	I would like to change that.
Harold:	If they don't go to school, could they do housework?
Teacher:	On the whole whenever I have been taking a class they have been reasonably good. On one occasion Tony, Raymond and Harold had been making a nuisance of themselves and I had to chuck them out. All the others are really quite good.
John:	Children have been coming to the 'Ministry of Works' when they have not been going to school.
Speaker:	I suggest that we should get over the difficulty in some other way. Is there any way other than throwing them out?
Bobby:	I think they should be kept in.
Bob:	If they did cause a disturbance make them

write five hundred lines and fine them if they
don't do them."

*A few weeks later a new Head Teacher arrived. He (Paul) opened
the discussion:*

"H.T.: I feel it rather presumptuous to make any
suggestions at the moment but there are some
things about which I want to tell you. At the
moment teachers here do not know who will
come to their lesson. You have decided that the
school should be voluntary and all I am concerned about is that the work should be
organized. For instance, supposing Lillian
does not know how many are coming to the
cookery class she does not know what to prepare. Another point, in a subject like Maths
you cannot learn very much unless you come
regularly, so it seems that if people are going
to come to Maths at all, they should come for a
fairly long time, at least a week. We should
avoid having two things going on at the same
time so that people who like both don't have to
miss one. It seems that teachers should ask
you what you want to do and notes will be
taken of names and classes will be arranged to
fit in with the people who want to do it. I
think that there is one difficulty at present:
that if we ask you now what you want to do
you would not quite know as you don't really
know what the subject is about, how it is
going to be taken or the person who is going
to take it. I am going to suggest that next week
we have a trial and we start to do all the things
we are prepared to do at definite times e.g.
9.30 Maths etc. You will be quite free to go
to any of these things and at the end of the
week we will ask you which you want to stick
to and then we will arrange a timetable.

John:	The question about how many will be coming to class: I think it is obvious that not many people come to Maths and a lot to Woodwork and Art and at English there is a fair amount. We could ask Matthew or Pauline.
Bob:	Did Paul bring up about P.T.?
Speaker:	That would come in with games but it really has not been mentioned. Are there any other ideas?
Bob:	How long are we going to have games for?
Speaker:	That will be arranged by Paul.
Teacher:	In reply to John the fact that we should already know how many people come to each subject is quite true but we really do not know who these people will be and Paul's point is that he would like to know who is coming.
Peter:	I would suggest that he finds out after each lesson who is coming the next day.
John:	I would like to put forward the suggestion as to whether we could do P.T. before breakfast. This would save staff time later in the day.
Teacher:	As regards getting up before breakfast I think it would not be practical, as you know the bother there is in getting people up.
Bob:	If we had P.T. in the morning it would be for the people who want to do it and they would get up.
John:	That is why I suggested it because I want to do it.
Speaker:	Are all the people in this house in favour of P.T. before breakfast?
Lillian:	Need we have a vote as it's only for the people who want to do it.
Teacher:	As all the subjects are going to be voluntary and the times to be decided on by the teachers anyway, surely P.T. should be left as it is, the same as the rest of the subjects?
Bob:	Could we be divided into houses, i.e. teams?

Kim:	In my last school in India we were divided into four houses. Couldn't we have it here?
John:	I think we could give the houses local names.
Teacher:	Regarding this matter of houses, i.e. dividing up into separate groups, it would bring about opposition between groups and most of the trouble is now caused by rivalries and what we want is more co-operation rather than competition.
Lillian:	We are not a big enough group for that anyway.
John:	It could be two houses. As regards Matthew's (teacher) suggestion, there would be competition for sport etc. and that would wipe out the other sort of competition like fighting. We would do things to uphold the honour of the house and as the little ones might get cheated we could have a housemaster.
Dick:	I don't think the staff should be brought into fighting.
John:	We could have captains then.
June:	It is most likely to be John.
Bob:	If we are going to have four teams we could have four leaders.
Speaker:	If this is passed these points can be decided later.
Teacher:	I suggest that this matter of houses is not relevant to the subject tonight and should be left to a later meeting.

I think that if you look at the other schools where there are houses, you will see that the reason for having houses is not to have competition, but because they are too large to run activities. This does not apply here. |
| Speaker: | I agree with Mr. Banks that we should adjourn this subject until the next debate. The question is whether we are satisfied with the time-table Paul read out. Can we have a vote on it?" |

Bill himself was convinced that the children he had round him needed to be persuaded to take the fullest advantage of whatever education could be made available to them. He knew that it could provide indispensable weapons for these children who had no backgrounds worth speaking of to sustain them in the harsh battles of life. He wanted to provide them with at least as much as the Central School in Caernarvon had provided for the children in Wales. He believed also that if the 'home' side of things at Alresford was free and relaxed the majority of the children would soon become secure enough in themselves to face the 'frustration' of education. This could be reduced to a minimum by making the lessons as interesting as possible. It could also be reduced by making sure that all the punishing aspects of school life were eliminated. Whatever punishment was going to be administered was going to come from the meeting and be from the whole community, not from any individual member of the staff.

It was only a matter of time until the children, with some encouragement from Bill it must be admitted, came to see that compulsory classes were really the best idea *for them*. They voted for it. Only two reservations were made. One was that there should be no lessons during the first week of each term. This was to give children a little time to get used to the idea of lessons and to get a little fed up with having to provide all their own entertainment! Secondly some elasticity in the interpretation of the word compulsory was to be allowed (Bill had in mind especially new children or some with pronounced difficulties). A compulsory time-table has remained in force ever since both at Alresford and at Childscourt.

Meanwhile the development of the community was beginning to follow the lines already established at the hostels. Bill himself was becoming more and more aware of the extent to which his work was growing from his fundamental principles. These may be briefly described as socialist, humanist and agnostic. The application of the first must have been obvious from the beginning in the essentially democratic procedure followed, in Bill's continual emphasis on the need to give all children a *really* fair start in life, and in the deliberate cultivation of a sense of using and sharing property together. The second may not have been quite so obvious, except in the general sense in which the purpose of a humanist ran through the work, but it was this humanist element in his thinking and feeling which enabled him to stumble upon one of the most important needs of a high percentage of disturbed children. They cannot be moralized at. They need a relaxation rather than a tightening up of the conscience.

Bill had felt a hardness in the way in which conventional morality is enforced, even while often agreeing with many of its aims. He believed that the pressure of moral training and moral expectations was frequently too great for the constitutions of many children. He felt convinced that if this pressure could be taken off children many of those who had developed emotional troubles would find speedy relief and would actually come nearer to achieving desirable standards of behaviour as a result. He believed that the child's natural desire to live with his fellow human beings provided a better motive for good behaviour than fear of any abstract principle or precept. He really meant to put this into practice. He showed no trace of the horror which teachers frequently exhibit, sometimes hypocritically, at lying or swearing or cheating or stealing. In fact he made it very clear to the children that all normal adults have at one time or another done all these things and that many of them continue to do some of them all their lives. At the same time he guided them towards finding a real morality in social life. In forming their own community he knew that they would discover real reasons for not doing most of the things which moralists condemned on abstract or religious grounds.

Bill had too often seen children who felt isolated and afraid of their own actions to use the weapons of morality against them. He believed that they needed a drastic relaxation of conscience if they were ever going to achieve realistic standards of behaviour in practice. He was quite plainly a master hand at jolting the standards which children had formed in their minds. He tells of one instance which made a deep impression on him shortly after he had arrived at Alresford. A boy on the threshold of adolescence wandered up to him. His face was pale and his eyes had a miserable look in them, a touch of violence that seemed as if it might break out at any moment, not a violence that was there because it was part of his nature but a violence born of desperation. During the course of snatches of conversation around the school the boy finally got round to telling Bill straight out about his trouble: masturbation. "Oh, you don't want to worry too much about that, son," came Bill's casual reply, "everybody does that at times. Can't talk about it now. I've got to rush out and see that the other kids are not putting up the new camp too near the garden. . . ."

The boy had thought he was alone in doing some desperately evil thing which no other good human being would do and yet now the head of his new school was more interested in some kids who were putting up a tent than in his evil doing! From that day on his face began to brighten up and the look of desperation in his eyes gradually faded. It impressed Bill because the connection between his remark to the boy and his sudden improvement was so obvious. There was no other possible way of interpreting it. He had often worked instinctively in the past and not been really sure of what had caused what. This clear demonstration of the cause of improvement was to make an important impression on his interpretation of his own techniques. It has to be remembered of course that he had already created the atmosphere and confidence which enabled the boy to come up to him in the first place and speak about his problem.

Bill's agnosticism led him to resist any attempt to force him to include an act of Christian worship in the daily life of the school. Studying the Bible and discussing some of the social implications of the teachings of Jesus Christ he had no objection to at all so long as it went with a readiness to think, question and doubt. The idea of a compulsory act of worship in which all taking part didn't honestly and sincerely believe horrified him. The fact of children being made to stand in rows saying the same Christian prayers day after day, like 'the vain repetitions of the heathen', was an insidious attack on the child's natural intelligence, if not actually a form of brainwashing.

He felt positive that such compulsory religion, and the hypocrisy that went with it, must have a confusing and damaging effect on a young, developing mind which had struggled from babyhood, even through its phantasy, to come to terms with the real world. He met this confusion again and again in individual children and he observed a clear link between it and their emotional condition. He noticed once again that by relaxing the demands of religion, a distinct improvement came about in the emotional condition and behaviour of many children.

One small boy had heard the story of Abraham's sacrifice of Isaac and had seriously believed that the same would happen to him. He had not dared to mention it and had lived under a cloud of fear as a result. As the framework of religious belief was not maintained at Alresford and doubts were sown in his mind, the secret fear of what would be done to him naturally diminished. A girl from a very strong Roman Catholic family arrived. She made her dolls and teddy bears go through all the rituals of religion which she herself hated. With the relaxation of religious demands, however, this began to abate. Unfortunately she was withdrawn from the school in the course of this improvement because she was not being given the religious instruction required by her parents and church. A few children from fanatically evangelical homes had similar experiences. They were troubled by incontinence rather than compulsive rituals. Many of the children were suffering from religious disturbances to a lesser degree and clearly benefited from the absence of religious demands of any kind.

Bill wished, however, to provide something positive in the place of compulsory religion. He felt that, apart from teaching about religions and about the life of Christ in particular, he should foster an understanding of, and a feeling for life as a whole and encourage a sense of respect for the universe. He believed that children should learn something of the known continuity of life. In order to teach this he started with the process of evolution and the development of man, a subject which he had magnificently illustrated in his own classroom at Alresford. This helped children to get their own position in life in what he considered a sound perspective and fitted in well with his ideas on moral and religious 'relaxation'. Disturbed children far more than others, he felt convinced, desperately needed to be freed of any unnecessary demands upon them. If they could grow to feel a sense of wonder at the universe, an appreciation of culture and man's achievements, a sensitivity to art and nature, Bill had no doubt that if there were any religious ideas within them they would grow in a much more healthy manner in that soil than in the fears and disturbances of infantile and adolescent problems. He felt that every effort should be made to dissociate the latter from children's attitudes to religion and morality. He had already felt utterly convinced that at least ninety per cent of the children sent to him could recover in the sort of free atmosphere he was trying to create and were in no need of any kind of special psychological treatment.

A community in which to unwind and develop—that was the keynote of what Bill had provided in Wales and was now struggling to provide at Alresford. His own toleration enabled the children to show an unusual degree of it in their relations with others. This was noticed by every visitor to the school and was always the occasion of some surprise. Tom Thompson, a B.B.C. reporter who came during the early days of the school's life, noticed an amazing natural acceptance of unusually regressive behaviour. "Some of the boys took me out to the camps. . . 'We get in there when it's raining', one of them told me. I noticed that he carried a toy pistol and had on a jester's cap of coloured paper, but nobody remarked on this unusual headgear for the middle of the day." On the same day Tom Thompson was impressed by a group of children who had met him at the door. They had asked him his name and he had replied, 'Tom'. "From then on," he said, "I was Tom to everybody." If he'd said, 'Mr. Thompson' he would have been 'Mr. Thompson' to everybody. The children seemed to him, and to many others, to be able to feel and respect adults' wishes without any trace of affectation. This was just another aspect of the tolerant spirit which prevailed among the children and to which Mr. Thompson referred in such glowing phrases as "an atmosphere of Christ-like toleration prevails".

It was undoubtedly this new-found sense of toleration which helped individual children to make adjustments in their own homes or foster homes, even sometimes with intolerant parents or guardians. In this connexion Bill refused to take up the frequently encountered view that the blame for these children's condition lies with the parents. He felt that most of the parents were themselves unhappy and not so much to be blamed as to be pitied. They themselves, like their children, were constantly subjected to social and economic pressures and were the victims of the same 'false morality' which affected their children. He met them regularly at end of term plays, open days etc., and I think the majority appreciated that Bill was doing something good for their children and had a sympathetic, rather than a critical attitude towards themselves.

Bill always gave the children positive encouragement to act tolerantly towards their parents, even if they knew or thought they knew them to be in the wrong. He encouraged them to want to give a good impression of their school. What he did not do was to say or imply that any sense of absolute rightness should be attached to parents merely because they were parents. He avoided studiously any involvement in the details of home relationships, but by and large he managed to please parents and to convince them that their children were getting the *best* and not the worst of education. It was here that a certain appearance of 'richness' again played an important part. He has been able to achieve this to a high degree at Childscourt and has noticed the visible signs of pleasure on the parents' faces. Once again he believed that he was aiming a pretty shrewd blow at their sense of deprivation and removing one cause for some of them to nag at their children during the school holidays. Occasionally, however, as in the case of one ten-year-old boy who was receiving quite blatant 'love letters' from his foster mother, describing the white wedding they would have and other almost unbelievable descriptions of nuptial delights, Bill took drastic action against parents. He forbade the foster mother to come even within the school grounds to see the boy. If she wanted to claim her right to take the boy out she could meet him outside the school. Bill made no secret of his opinion of the woman when talking to the boy who was probably more influenced by the fact that he, Bill, forbade the mother to come into the school than by anything that was said.

As the group at Alresford began to grow in strength and numbers and to start developing an effective nucleus of children who had some understanding of Bill's aims and were loyal to the school, the Honorary Psychiatrist began to make her visits felt. She interviewed individual children and seemed to drive them back to a state of nervousness and uncertainty which frequently created fresh trouble within the school community and certainly hindered development. Bill asked if these visits could cease and gave his word that he would refer to her any children with whom he himself found special difficulty. This suggestion was emphatically rejected by the Committee and he was given firm instructions to give his full co-operation to the psychiatrist and to assist her in catching individual children for the interviews which took place in the small room which was also her bedroom during her weekend visits. He began to find that unsuitable new members of staff were being sent into the school and that a high proportion of very badly disturbed children were being accepted. He was not being consulted on these matters and he felt that it was important that the majority of the children should be of the kind who would benefit from the type of community life he aimed to provide. Relations with the Committee became so strained that he finally resigned in 1951.

After a short spell in charge of a hostel in Bedfordshire, Bill found himself receiving urgent requests from the Committee of Alresford Place School, begging him to return. Nobody had seemed able to do the job he had done. The school had been badly knocked about. Bill returned to Alresford on a visit and only agreed to continue his work there after laying down very exacting conditions to the Committee. He was to be on the Committee himself, to have the final say in the choice of staff and no children were to be sent without reference to him.

After lunch one day not long after returning to Alresford four of the biggest boys, who had been accepted during his absence, swaggered into his classroom where he was sitting typing a letter. One of them stepped forward and looking down and shuffling into a challenging attitude, said, "We're going out this afternoon". In an instant Bill saw what they were doing and instinctively felt that the one thing that they must not do on that afternoon was to go out. They were intent on attack. Bill attacked first and before they had time to think what was happening he'd knocked their spokesman flat on the ground. "What you going to do about your bloody friend?" he asked in the same tone of voice as that in which they'd announced their intentions for the afternoon. "There are odd occasions when you have to step out of line and act against all your principles and if you don't all your work will be destroyed," said Bill afterwards. In his opinion that occasion was one of them and in fact it was mainly a matter of self-defence. "They were big powerful boys intent on destroying me and the school. For a moment I felt like a cornered fox taking the only way out."

As the year went by Bill regained his control of the children, things became calmer once more and the community was gradually settling down and becoming relaxed as it had been before Bill's departure. Unfortunately, interference began again in spite of the terms on which Bill

c

returned. It was becoming plain that things were never going to turn out really satisfactorily. At the end of the year Bill sent in his annual progress report to the Committee. One or two sections of it will help to indicate the way things were going and even more important the way in which Bill's own thinking was developing on fundamental issues. The problem of staff with psychological interests was arising again. Bill felt more convinced than ever that far too much attention was being concentrated on the disturbed children among the pupils, in consequence of which their disturbances were actually becoming worse. He was in a good position to see over a long period the effects of children having been interviewed and in some cases treated by psychiatrists. Like Barbara Wootton after her experiences in the courts he became doubtful of the value of this kind of treatment for the majority of disturbed children. He felt certain that unless children were in a very bad condition it was wrong to do anything that might cause them to think of themselves as mental patients. He was anxious also about the effects of social workers and teachers who attempted anything that looked to the children like psychiatry.

There had been rumours in some quarters about Bill only managing to keep order by the use of hidden violence. Bill felt it was absolutely necessary to make his position clear and to dispel any exaggerated additions to the truth. The report began with this subject: "We entered this work twelve years ago holding the firm conviction that corporal punishment, used either as deterrent to mischief or as a stimulus to effort, was both barbarous and senselessly stupid. In the light of our experience during that time we find that we have no cause to change this belief, in fact we are more firmly convinced than ever. However, it should be stressed that until the children have been with us long enough to relax tension and until the community government becomes really effective, we do, when no other course presents itself, forcibly restrain badly disturbed children, who are in a primitive state of hate against the whole world and beyond reason, from being cruel to each other, or to animals, or interfering malignantly in the peaceful pastimes of their companions . . . Until the meaning and effect of community law is understood by all the children and until the law to protect both weak and strong alike is functioning efficiently, the children must have something or someone they can depend on and who will actively defend them against the often senselessly cruel acts of their contemporaries."

Co-education and the special need for it among children whose emotions are disturbed is again stressed. The report goes on to make Bill's position clear not only with regard to psychiatry but with regard to the basic practical problems and difficulties of scientific observation of children. "If the personalities in daily contact with the children are there because they have real pity and understanding for these bewildered and apprehensive children who are approaching the threshold of adult life and responsibility, then the chance of successful development is real. However, I am very much aware that, if we are to do any lasting good and to lay down principles for the future treatment of badly disturbed children, we must accept the research aspect of our work. I am of course eager and willing to co-operate with psychiatry with that end in view. But could not this be done without the children, once they have been interviewed for admission and placed in our care, being made to feel that they are 'different' and therefore apart from other children? They are different we know because of the things that have happened to them, but should they be allowed to know that we think so? It must be very unsettling to a frightened child to be aware that it is under constant surveillance by staff, welfare workers, psychologists, psychiatrists and others.

"Each generation passes through the normal 'abnormalities' of adolescence when they feel all hands, feet and pimples; experience strong frightening urges and even stronger revulsions, as well as terrible feelings of lassitude. The majority grow and develop quite normally and there is a possibility that we may be losing our sense of proportion when our eyes are glued to the microscope examining human reactions. We must consider how terrifying it must be to the children when they realize that so many people are interested in their private urges and the physical disabilities brought on by adolescence. I would suggest that the idea of allowing children to work out their problems in a therapeutic, and therefore an apparently normal boarding school environment, subject only to unobtrusive observation, should be considered. If the visiting psychiatrists, social workers and others in official connexion with the school mixed with the children and staff as friends, and not as officials with other intent, we should then be able to obtain the necessary data for research purposes, perhaps more completely for that reason."

The report ends with a plea to allow children to be 'themselves': "In conclusion what level of behaviour, intellect or creative attainment do we require our children to reach, or is it simply that we want them to conform and accept the moral values of our time? If this last is true, are these moral standards beyond criticism? Perhaps we should do the sensible thing and give all children the opportunity to answer these questions themselves by allowing them to develop as individuals in an environment where certain basic principles are observed which protect them from exploitation in any form, and from the itch of almost all adults to mould them into some pre-conceived pattern of their own."

Looking back over this period, we can see how Bill developed, under conditions of terrible strain which have scarcely been touched upon here, a strong bias against psychiatry. There was an obvious danger that he would generalize from his unfortunate experience with the particular psychiatrist on the school committee but I do not think that he was doing this. It must be plain that he was taking into account the effects on children of all the psychiatrists from the counties who sent children to Alresford. I believe that it is important to remember that right through his work he always encountered a small minority of very badly disturbed children who could not respond to his social treatment. The disturbances of most of these, it may be assumed, resulted from some failure in their very early relationships with their parents. Bill would not disagree with the general psychoanalytic view that *in those cases* it is necessary to go back to those early stages, that only by a transference on to the analyst, who can re-enact the 'drama' with the parents and bring out of it a different result, can a cure be effected. Bill believed that this kind of fundamental emotional disturbance which manifests itself in the various forms of neurosis is not widespread. There is an enormous range of emotional problems (which are listed in Appendix B of the Underwood Report) which emphatically do not come within the same category as the neurotic disturbances. An example is the case of the boy mentioned earlier, who believed that he should be sacrificed after hearing the story of Abraham and Isaac. In his case *a mistaken judgment* led to a terrible emotional paralysis. What needed to be put right in that instance was simply a mistaken judgment. Surely this is the case with a great many children's disturbances, and indeed this was the reason why Bill was able to succeed so well with the majority of children sent to him. It explains also why group therapy is especially effective. Children's mistaken judgments will be much more easily altered in a group than by the persuasion of an individual. There is no point in giving these children any idea that they are mentally ill because they are not. They are merely mistaken.

4

The Human Scene at Alresford

To visitors there was nothing very startling about Alresford at first sight. They noticed that children were rather polite in a natural way and most of them felt bound to comment to that effect. It didn't seem as if anyone had been telling the children to say 'please' and 'thank you' or warning them that they must open doors for visitors. They seemed just to do these things but in reality of course such behaviour had grown out of a very special kind of loyalty to the school. For many it was the first school they could stand being in. It was a refuge from the reactions of hostile forces they so often seemed to bring upon themselves and Bill made it quite plain to them that he wanted to form a community in which they could be sheltered from much of the harsh treatment of the outside world. He made no bones about telling them of the difficulties of keeping such a school going and he enlisted their wholehearted support for the job. They really wanted to give the best possible picture of their school to outsiders. Children might have arguments and rows within the school and do many things which in any other community would bring about their final rejection. In Alresford they knew that whatever they did, short of murder, their troubles would always blow over. They might get shouted at by teachers or house staff but they were sure that underneath they were still accepted. They would never again bring the whole machinery of law and order into action against themselves. I believe that they valued this safety and knew that Bill was 'on their side'. It was equally clear that they were on Bill's side in all the things he decided to fight against. Unfortunately the main conflict was with the school committee and the Honorary Psychiatrist.

My first visit to Alresford was at the beginning of September, 1956. I was going to occupy a room on the top landing right in the middle of the boys' dormitories. Nobody took too much notice of me when I arrived. "Some of the big boys'll give you a hand up with your baggage," said Bill and disappeared. They did and seemed to enjoy doing it as they struggled with various heavy suitcases and trunks up the ugly stone staircase of an otherwise rather splendid Georgian mansion. Diamond-mesh, thick wire netting, such as might be used at a kennels or a zoo, was fixed on to the banisters to prevent the children from flying over and breaking their necks on the red-ochred flag stones below. There was a central coldness about this part of the school which the bright, warming influence of all Bill's efforts elsewhere could never entirely overcome. His own sitting room, into which the children constantly edged their way or were allowed in to play with his four-year-old daughter, Joanna, was colourful and although warm and homely conveyed a touch of Georgian splendour through the antique furniture it contained. The art room was another very colourful part of the school and showed many signs of the hidden abilities of children whom society had rejected. Bill's own classroom was very bright and interesting, displaying much general cultural and historical material as well as a set of striking illustrations of the evolution of man. He regarded this as one of his great weapons in his battle against the effects of a false morality.

Some children like Gary started questioning right away. "What's he?" asked Gary, pointing to a prehistoric monster at the beginning of the series. "Oh, creatures like that wandered around the world before man started." "And who's he?" Gary went on, pointing to an ape-man further along the series. "He's one of the forefathers of man," Bill replied. "Cor struth," exclaimed Gary, "was 'e really one of my great grandfathers," and there was a touch of admiration in his voice, which showed how much he was affected. His five-year-old mind was bringing all the power of its intellect to bear on a new line of thought. That forefather was really rather a splendid fellow. Perhaps it's really all right to be rather a splendid fellow yourself, etc. etc.

It was the beginning of a moral revolution in Gary. He had been brought up in a world of very limited ideas and values and even at the tender age of five he was finding it difficult to fit in. Thus, although one of the smallest children in the school, Gary was to become the focal point in intellectual development at the school meeting for some time. He was always asking questions that raised big issues. You could almost see the processes of reasoning going on when Gary asked questions or when Bill said something that would provoke him to comment. There was a kind of determination in the way he held his head back and the way his glasses slanted on his nose when he stood up to say something, as well as a readiness to hesitate and be found wrong if necessary. He also ate well, possibly more than well, and became a natural vegetarian. As time went by his body developed a remarkable solidarity, never fatness, which added to the effect of that four-square stand he took up when he had a point of view to uphold or a more physical kind of dispute with some fourteen-year-old giant! His courage, tenacity and honesty which had made him a rebellious nuisance in his former school now played an important part in the school community. Small children needed great courage to bring up bullying at the school meetings because they were subjected to threats of what would happen afterwards. It was necessary to be the very reverse of a cowardly sneak and it was undoubtedly such children as Gary who helped to stamp out bullying at Alresford.

As I talked to Bill during my first week there I quickly began to learn some of his ideas on the actual lessons and on education generally. These will emerge more clearly in the next chapter on Childscourt but must be touched upon briefly here. He stressed what he believed to be the central theme of the school side of his work: "What these children need is to learn to concentrate. They need that very much more than knowledge of any particular subject. Other children in free schools may need to be left free to concentrate on the things which really interest them. I still believe in that kind of freedom. Those children will learn through it and learn all they need. If these children, however, are left free they simply seem to perpetuate their dissatisfactions. They don't seem to grow out of them as I once thought they would. They cannot concentrate even on the things that really interest them. That is the crux of our problem. They cannot get through to the point where they are able on their own at any rate, to gain the satisfaction necessary to spur them on to further achievement. Anything that gets them to that point clearly helps them." He went on to express his view that though the children were emotionally disturbed, it was not in most cases due to deep psychological causes, but to pressures in their environment which they found themselves unable to live up to. They laugh at the standards of many adults brought up in a sheltered environment because they know the harshness of real life in their own experience. "Get rid of the pressures and many of the standards which *to them* are meaningless and ninety per cent of them improve automatically."

After a week during which absolutely no enforced activities took place the morning arrived when the first lessons and the school meeting were about to take place. Immediately after breakfast the dining hall was cleared and all the children and staff made their way into it. They sat wherever they wished. Some of the kids even sprawled flat on the floor on their stomachs. Staff also just found somewhere to sit and often quickly became surrounded by a group of children. One of the children acted as clerk to the meeting and Bill arrived last of all with Joanna who always liked to come into the first meeting of the term. She was followed by Colonel, an enormous, shaggy, old English sheep dog, who had once won a prize in a popular newspaper for being dressed up as a cricketer, and by Kim, the siamese cat. When Bill had seated himself he raised his hand slightly and called out, "Right, shut up now." The noise which had been going on until then instantly subsided and thenceforth hardly a word was spoken out of place. I quickly sensed that the meeting was really a pretty sacred thing in the life of the school and that the majority of the children who had been there for any length of time had learnt to value it. I began to see the remarkable power which Bill held over it though it was not until later that I realized the full need for the control which at times of crisis he was prepared to use to hold the school together. I even wondered about the ethical propriety of it.

Hands went up around the room. The children were ready and eager to speak up for themselves. "Yes, Betsy," said Bill, "we'll start with you." "I want to charge Pamela for swiping my nightdress out of my case when we came back on Monday." "Did she well, er, remove it?" demanded Bill as chairman. "Well, no, not exactly." "Well, what did she do with it?" At that moment Pamela's hand shot up, "I never touched her bloody nightdress." Bill asked her to keep calm. "We don't want swearing in the meeting, at least we don't mind swearing but we want to keep calm and find out facts. Did anybody see Pamela 'swipe' Betsy's nightdress?" "Yes," piped up several voices, "she just lifted it up from the case and put it down again when she'd looked at it." "Oh," groaned some of the boys, "another one of the girls' arguments starting up already this term." "Yes," said Bill, "we don't want to waste the time of the meeting on these little things."

This brief episode illustrates one of the essential techniques in Bill's approach. He plays down the importance of such a traditional vice as swearing but at the same time he does not encourage it. He avoids bringing about a swing to the opposite. In a few cases these tremendous swings of the emotions may be necessary in a therapeutic situation but they are not, as Anna Freud has argued very forcefully in her book, *The Psychoanalytic Treatment of Children*, normally appropriate in a school situation. Violent swings of the emotions can be extremely damaging to a community, particularly to a community of unsettled children. It was this, I believe, that brought Bill into violent conflict with the psychiatric approach of the committee. He was in fact loosening things up but checking them as this was happening by an extremely subtle system of reactions. He never said to the boy who was masturbating, "Go off and masturbate. It's quite all right to do so." He merely gave the feeling that it would not be condemned. It was not of tremendous importance. After that the boy was somewhat relieved of his mental-emotional paralysis and free to sort out the problem for himself.

And this is the essence of Bill's approach that children should cure themselves, should in fact solve their own problem without too much adult investigation of the problem in itself. He used this approach of relaxing, without giving the go ahead for any kind of emotional reversal, for dealing with the whole range of religious and moral feelings. It came out constantly in innumerable little reactions and slight comments on things, which are almost impossible to recapture and put into any sort of systematic pattern. They were produced almost unconsciously and invariably had an element of surprise about them. They were not thought out or designed to bring about any particular psychological response. They sprang from a general way of thinking and were as unconscious as the movements of an experienced motorist. The advantage of Bill's methods was not only that he avoided dramatic swings of the emotional pendulum but also left individual children free to apply what each one needed to his own situation. One is reminded of D. W. Winnicott's well known remark in *The Child and the Outside World* (Tavistock Publications), "It's no use telling a group of boys that it's all right to masturbate because for one of them it may not be all right." Children could take what they needed and not be involved in self-pitying discussions of their individual problems in themselves. He often achieved his purposes by such slight remarks as, "I don't know, son, it's all right, I suppose." Nothing was ever unmercifully condemned but neither was adult sponsored freedom used to press a child into any course of action merely because that course of action was contrary to the prevailing morality. To convert it into Winnicott's terms, no group of boys would ever be made to feel that they ought to masturbate.

The meeting went on. One of the older boys, who was only too capable of getting into serious trouble himself but had a weighty manner when he felt himself to be bringing up important subjects at the meeting, raised his hand. "Yes, Cheesy?" Cheesy announced that he had a rather serious charge to bring against 'Packet', a small boy with a very strong tendency to get involved in incidents of violence and destruction and an uncontrollable temper which could be restrained by nothing once it was roused. "Packet's been throwing stones at Mr. Vasselini's clay pigeons," announced Cheesy.

"Now listen," said Bill, "I'm going to tell you something. I don't really mind about Mr. Vasselini's clay pigeons. But do you know what he'd really like? He'd like to have you kids in a row and take pot shots at you. He'd find it much better sport. He'd really enjoy potting off kids. I don't like all the hunting and shooting that goes on round here, but I want you kids to keep well away from the fence at the top of the grounds. The neighbours really quite like us now because we don't cause them too much trouble and we don't want to give them any cause to say things against us outside. We all want them to know that this is just a normal school. What shall we do about Packet?"

Hands shot up and answers came in turn: "I think Packet should lose his cinema." "I think he should do spuds for a week, Bill." "I think he should get a warning because its only the beginning of term and we can all watch him for a bit and see that he doesn't go over there," piped up Ginger, another small boy of Packet's age and size. "We've had three suggestions and now we'll vote on it. Ginger's idea seems to me a pretty good one, though. We don't want to punish him. We only want to stop him and we only want to do that because if he goes on he can do harm to all of us."

The new children soon learnt that the meeting wasn't just somewhere to run off to in order to tell a tale on someone else you didn't like. "Don't waste the time of the meeting on these little things," Bill frequently remarked. At other times he would let apparently trivial things go on. Some small charge was brought up. "It's a spite charge, Bill," remarked Willy, "Tom's had it in for Cheesy all week. He's even been trying to mess up his garden." "Anybody else seen him doing that?" Several voices piped up, "Yes, Bill." Very careful judgments of tones of voice, of expressions on faces etc., is needed to decide if the witnesses are really genuine. Sometimes Bill suspects a bit of a 'gang up' and says so. The matter is often dropped. No sanction may have been carried out but a number of children are set thinking about what they are really doing. The merely plausible children and the trouble makers have to reveal themselves in the end.

Work in the classroom was extremely difficult. The teacher was confronted with a very different situation from that which he would face in a normal Secondary Modern school. The classes at Alresford and at Childscourt were really a concentration of the few persistent 'trouble makers' who are found in almost every lower stream class. Their surface reactions against teachers and school are very quickly dispelled. They become in most cases within the matter of a term very much nicer children to deal with. Their resistances to teachers and school as such almost disappear. Their resistances to the actual subject matter of lessons, which makes real demands on their powers of thought and concentration, do not disappear nearly so easily. This often makes it hard for the casual visitor to judge the academic work of the school. He sees the good superficial attitudes of the children and is therefore inclined to underestimate the deeper resistances. The teacher finds that these children are perfectly all right so long as they are doing some simple repetitive type of work such as copying from the blackboard or textbooks or doing large numbers of simple sums of the same kind. It soon becomes obvious that they are 'kidding' themselves that they are making normal educational progress. They are trying to give themselves the feeling that they are in a normal school without having to do the hard work involved in learning. If they are faced with real work they will use every possible 'go slow' tactic to divert the teacher's attention. They will come without pens, they will be short of a book, they will want something or other marked that doesn't really need marking, they will bring up arguments between themselves and every kind of imaginable red herring until the teacher is at his or her wit's end. He feels like tearing his hair out. He knows that he can perhaps shut the children up by force but he cannot make them learn by force. He has to think about so many little incidental things that he cannot keep his mind on the lesson itself. This makes it very hard to operate a progressive curriculum or scheme of work either with a class or with individuals within a class. If a subject is chosen for a set of lessons the children are liable to groan, "Oh no, not so and so again," or "You're always doing so and so." They will do this even with a subject entirely of their own choice. A boy can be offered an illustrated encyclopaedia. He will glance through the pages during the last five minutes of a lesson. When he is offered it the following week his comment is, "Er, I don't want that. I've read it." The characteristic of most of these children is extreme impatience. It is this that makes ordinary class work, even with very small classes, very hard to organize.

At Alresford, because of the frequent changes of staff and the regular upheaval that followed the psychiatric interviews, it was impossible to get children really going on an educational programme. The teacher had to be thankful if the children were reasonably quiet, did a bit of reading and writing and achieved some sort of concentration on games which involved elements of thought and calculation. It was to the teacher's credit if he could get the children to pursue these to the end without wanting to throw the board up into the air at the first signs of the possibility of losing. This I believe was not realized by visitors and inspectors.

On one occasion an inspector from one of the Local Education Authorities which sent children to the school visited my class. She considered that the work going on in the school was much too haphazard and asked if she could speak to one of the boys in the class. Her conversation, which went very well, lasted for about ten minutes. "Yes," she said, "my conversation with him proves that a consistent and progressive scheme of work could be carried out over the course of weeks, terms and years. They are quite well behaved children and could easily be trained to take a progressive series of lessons in all school subjects." I disagreed of course, and argued that you have to be with the children for a reasonable period of time to know what they can and can't do. "Who was that bloody old cow?" asked Robert, the boy she'd been talking to, the moment she'd gone out. "She's just like one of the prying old bags in the school I bolted from." And he snarled viciously and went on about her for half the lesson. "I was only bloody polite to 'er because she was a visitor and I don't want to do any bloody harm to the school, but I'd like to go and tell 'er what she could do with 'er questions. . . ."

The teacher at Alresford was almost bound to experience with some surprise the almost total lack of any powers of concentration in the children when he attempted to take them outside for a nature study walk or any sort of novel activity not on the normal timetable, which he would naturally assume would be of interest to the children and give them satisfaction. On a nature study walk they would very quickly run wild in various directions. A class had once begged and pestered me to show them the various parts of a motor car. I took them outside and raised the bonnet of my car to show and explain the things in which they had expressed the keenest interest. Within three minutes four of them had tried to pull various parts off the car. Others had tried to run off and do different things. Their interest in the car as such had ceased as rapidly as the interest of the boy who thought he'd read the encyclopaedia after flicking the pages over in five minutes.

This is the core of the problem with most emotionally disturbed children and this was why Bill emphasized their need to achieve concentration and the satisfactions of accomplishment. It must be noted however that the kind of behaviour which occurred with the car only did so during what was thought of as a lesson. A car could be left standing outside the garage for a week and normally none of the children would dream of touching it. In that case it came within the sphere of social behaviour, and the social behaviour of the children was remarkably good. The same was true with gardens. It naturally seemed a good idea for each child to have and look after his own little patch of garden. What could be better? What could provide a better sense of accomplishment? But it did not work out like that. Interest evaporated very quickly. Nature was too slow for them. They began to want to destroy each other's gardens during gardening lessons. The ownership of gardens seemed to arouse jealousy and envy. Gardens also provided an ideal opportunity for children to get their own back secretly on those who they thought had wronged them. It was frequently brought up at meetings that every single plant had been pulled out of somebody's garden. It was sad but it was obvious that privately owned gardens were not going to be a source of productive satisfactions.

Despite all these difficulties with these children I believe that it would be a mistake to describe the condition of the majority of them as pathological. One could feel this when one contrasted their condition with that of a small minority whose difficulties did really seem to have deep roots. Most of them seemed to have difficulties arising from pressures related to judgments and standards, stated or implicit, in their former environments rather than from early traumatic experiences. Bill's work showed clearly how quickly they changed when their environment changed. Even in regard to the problems of learning, the difficulty was not usually related to one subject or one aspect of a subject. It usually seemed due to a general kind of 'jumpiness' which simply made learning anything almost impossible. This rule appeared to be proved by the exception. One boy of twelve could not learn more than the first five letters of the alphabet despite a good deal of individual tuition by various teachers. He was probably a case for psychiatry. But the others were not and should never have been made to feel they were 'cases' because it plainly aggravated their jumpiness. Exceptions like this amounted to no more than half a dozen in the whole school and yet all the children felt that they were in some sense psychological cases. Bill had to go to somewhat unprofessional lengths to try to eradicate this impression from their minds.

'Podge' was another notorious character in the school. He always wore visible braces pulled up much too tight to give a somewhat obscene appearance to the short grey pants beneath them. He was an expert at stirring up trouble in class in ways that almost passed belief. He had an extraordinary capacity for eliciting either anger or guilty tittering laughter from children around him and gave an impression of incredible depravity in a community where very little was really thought of as depraved. It would need an Apuleius to describe it adequately. On one occasion there had been a disturbance in class which I had found it difficult to account for. One girl was wildly angry. The rest of the class were getting fits of uncontrollable giggling. Podge was working at his sums. " 'Ave I been good?" he asked in characteristic fashion as he left the classroom half bent over and ready to run. It came out at the meeting that Podge had been whispering, "Marion's mum's got a face like the backside of a turnip." Another great delight of his was charging other children with "twanging me braces". He could rely on causing trouble with that or at least getting a tittering laugh from the other children. What he appeared to like best was rushing up to other children and screaming "Fanny's knickers" at them and trying to involve them in his own strange high-pitched fits of hysterical laughter. He was a regular and voluntary attender at the sessions of the visiting psychiatrists. Bill felt passionately that it was these visits which prevented him from helping Podge to become more normal in his behaviour. Eventually he became socially ostracised by the majority of the children.

Bob was a different sort of character altogether. He was a real cockney and had all the cockney aggressiveness which is so often overlooked by sentimental cockney lovers. He'd thrown a brick at Bill on the first day he arrived and had a strong right arm with which he knew how to terrorize other children, though he used it with some discrimination. When I first went to Alresford he couldn't read although he was nearly eleven. Suddenly he decided that he wanted to and forced every teacher to pay special attention to him during every lesson. "Git on with it," he'd say and, "Er, shud up," he'd shout at the rest of the class, "or I'll kick yer teeth in at the end of the lesson." He became a shining example of ruthless determination in the matter of reading and startled everybody once he'd decided that it wasn't daft to struggle through the reading books for five-year-olds. Within the term he was reading fluently.

His father was a 'totter' and unfortunately Bob's great aim in life was to follow in his footsteps. In the meantime, so long as he had to remain at school, he undertook many of the rough jobs such as looking after the boilers. They suited him and he showed a very praiseworthy sense of responsibility. Unfortunately his admiration for his Dad's work was almost bound to land him into trouble, despite all Bill's efforts to make him see the situation.

Some years later, long after he'd left school and grown up, he and his Dad were 'collecting' lead and proceeded to jail together. It was a tragic pity. Society can find a place for, and is glad of, boys of such calibre in times of war. It ought to be sufficiently flexible and magnanimous in its legal system not to crush them in times of peace. Bob was doing no more than fulfilling himself in going out on that 'job' with his Dad, like the sons of fishermen in the Pacific islands, who follow their fathers out into dangerous waters. He did it through a process of natural identification, natural morality. He was not committing a crime. It was an adventure and both he and his Dad despised the un-adventurous. Bob might have come through to safety and found a different outlet for his spirit if he'd been at Childscourt, where Bill's influence was not overshadowed by conflicting forces, instead of at Alresford.

The connection with bad influences during the holidays was a grave problem and the conflict between Bill and these outside influences was constantly blurred by the internal conflict between the committee and Bill. Bob's friend Harry, known to all the children as 'Poker Nose' because he always poked his nose into everything that was going on, had almost gone too far during the Summer holidays with two slightly younger boys. They had something to boast about when they arrived back at school. "Did you read about that big hold up on the North Circular road. They got away didn't they? Well, we were up in the trees watching for them. That was how they did it." It seemed true all right. It needed something strong to oppose it. It seemed to show a kind of 'smart Alec' attitude that so many of the children had acquired. Bill felt that one of the most urgent needs was to try to educate them out of the notion that they could 'trick society'. He knew that it was extremely hard to do. It seemed to be a kind of blind ingrained hope which was scarcely susceptible to any form of intelligent reasoning. He knew that this 'education' had to be accomplished without suggesting that society was in the right. He felt sure that nothing could be done without taking the side of the offenders *against society*. And he meant this in no sentimental sense.

He often rounded on the children for the stupidity of this belief in the possibility of being able to trick society. He would not hesitate to use very strong language indeed to express his impatience with the smart Alecs. The language removed any impression that he was speaking from a moral point of view. He was determined that what he was saying was based only on their own point of view. Lots of things could be done in the school which would have caused severe bother outside. "You know that if you did that outside they'd get you in five minutes for it, you stupid little sod," was a typical kind of comment Bill would make. It was never aimed to put the child in the wrong in relation to a society which was right. In this way he often got through to

83

the children, particularly to the bigger boys who, after doing some job in the evening, would congregate in the kitchen for a cup of cocoa before going to bed. Discussions then would often go on until far into the night.

It was here that some of the best work with the older boys could be done for it was at this time, all sitting round the kitchen table or standing with their back to the old kitchen range, that they began to reveal and discuss their *real* aspirations. The masks were removed and real wishes were discussed. Bill tried always to bring them to see the reality of what they could achieve and to see the reality of what society was like. He knew that they had to face these realities. Many liberal-minded people might have preferred to have discussed a theoretical outline of what society should be like and perhaps only succeeded in increasing the children's chip on their shoulders, thereby making them more likely to carry out some impulsive action and land themselves in trouble. Sometimes this kind of subject came up at the meeting after children had committed some offence. I can recall Bill once speaking to a couple of children in the meeting in tones of complete and utter despair: "I can just see you two sitting in a prison cell telling each other how smart you'd both been, how marvellously you'd fooled the police until you were caught. You'll get so carried away with your own smartness that you'll forget you're in clink."

Bill believed that while the laws which govern the activities of children and teenagers are as harsh as they are at present, they must be prepared to face them. It is just no use speaking to children sympathetically if it is going merely to increase their feeling of being wronged and thereby inflame the feelings which make them want to break out irrationally against society. He argues also that there is a certain streak of unrealism in the work of some psychiatrists who loosen up children emotionally in the clinical situation but do not fit them to face the sometimes harsh and inconsistent decisions of the law. His really shocking conflicts with the psychiatrically orientated committee may have biassed his judgments against psychiatry. But sometimes it is only through highly one-sided judgments that we see the faults in well-established procedures.

At Alresford it was impossible for Bill to make the authoritative impression he wished to make on the parents of the children at the school, because his authority was in such open conflict with that of the committee. He met most of the families of the children at the school plays and at various end-of-term events. He sometimes kept children on as junior members of the steff if he thought they could be useful and would benefit from the extended period in the school environment, especially if the homes were completely unsuitable and it looked as though the Authorities could not provide any alternative. Many of his past pupils visited from time to time and almost all kept in contact by post.

Right the way through however he believed that his work was being unnecessarily frustrated. He did not get suitable staff or suitable equipment and quite a number of the children accepted were not within the range he could hope to manage with the degree of success he had achieved in North Wales. After unspeakable difficulties and much reluctance, he and Lillian decided to hand in their resignation in the Summer of 1960. The school closed just over a year later.

5

Childscourt—
Its Beginnings and Development

What had truly been a nightmare experience was over. Bill had cut himself adrift, determined to start up his own school and confirmed in his belief that committees are the ultimate evil. For a year almost he struggled to borrow money and to find a suitable home for his purposes. It was a time of severe credit squeeze and money was very difficult to come by. He eventually received help from friends of mine, who were interested in the project, and the Old Rectory at Long Bredy in Dorset provided reasonably suitable premises and was obtained for a moderate price. Preparations were rushed ahead during the Spring and Summer of 1961 in order to have the school ready to open at the beginning of the school year in September. Expenditure had run much higher than anticipated and the school opened under the cloud of an almost crippling financial debt.

On September the fourth the first child arrived clutching the hand of her social worker. The magnificent entrance hall of the school, which Bill had been severely criticised for spending so much money on, made her hold her breath for a moment or two, visibly gasp, while within the question must have flashed across her mind: was this a school or was it the palace of her fairy godmother? The decor certainly had an impressive effect on deprived children and their parents too if they happened to come along. Children continued to come in ones and twos. Local authorities were undoubtedly interested in the way in which the school was developing.

It looked as if there must be plenty of money behind it but in fact the position at the bank was getting steadily worse. Expenditure on the few children who had arrived far outran the amounts expected in fees. I had daily letters from Bill telling me of the constant demands of creditors. "We cannot go on for long as we are," he wrote, "when we feel terrible if we buy even a packet of cigarettes." From the friends who had backed the venture I also received almost daily letters. "Are you sure we ought to go on?" was the constant question. I knew that the school was getting deeper into debt and we had only promises of children from local authorities on whose fees we should have to rely in order to get over the initial financial difficulties.

By half-term Bill's letters began to sound a slightly more hopeful note. "All is going well with the children, and it is encouraging to see Linda, one of the first pupils, responding so well, considering that almost every children's home in the South of England had failed to hold her, the cause of newspaper articles and questions by M.P.s in the House of Commons! Indeed I can say even at this early date that she is really a nice girl who has suffered from complete mis-understanding by adults hitherto in contact with her. . . . Each morning is a minor crisis on the financial front. Even my short forceful word of dismissal of any problem is lacking in strength! This morning I received my statement from the Bank. Two of my cheques are going to bounce this week."

Children began to arrive much faster during the second half of the term and by the end eleven children were on the books and definite bookings for the beginning of the following term could be relied upon to bring the total number up to fifteen, which according to my reckoning was the minimum number with which the school could be run with any hope of survival. Fifteen had become, in fact, the magic number. It satisfied Bill's financial supporters. It was possible to begin repaying the creditors and from then on the school showed a gradual improvement in its financial fortunes.

While all this was happening on what we had come to call the financial front, the real creative work within the school was forging ahead. It was done almost exclusively by Bill and Lillian in the early stages and in this hard and important sense they were its true founders. While the children were arriving only in ones and twos it was impossible to start a real school and pointless to begin the meetings. There were classes of course but they were fairly casual in the beginning. The real job was to get the children settled and to make them want to stay at the school. It had to be a home and at the same time be without much of the morality and many of the emotional demands of a home.

There is really amazingly little to describe about the beginnings of this new community. It didn't start with a bang like the Hostel at Bryn Conway. There was none of the drama of the internal conflict for power as at Alresford. To me, at least, it seemed to start with rather quiet whispers. During my frequent visits to deal with the financial side of things I remember picking my way through a seemingly contented little family of children (which grew a little faster than a normal family) to reach Bill's sitting room. They gave me cheerful hellos as they tore their eyes from the television screen for a few seconds. At all other times they were either at lessons, in bed or in some far corner of the grounds from which they gave me a distant wave.

Bill knew what to demand and what not to demand from individual children and if actual schooling was a little haphazard in those early stages, it was probably no disadvantage. It gave a tremendous sense of relaxation to the children and those who were there tend to look back upon it nostalgically as a golden age in their lives. Perhaps it was not quite so golden at the time but it was undoubtedly a good and easy time for them when they felt really free from all the pressures of school. And heaven knows they needed it. The case histories of the older children who arrived at this time were fairly startling, sprinkled with such comments as, "Turned out of, or absconded from, numerous children's homes and other institutions," "severe nymphomaniac at thirteen," "constant lying and thieving," "battered mother unconscious and laughed at it," "tried to burn down children's home," "ringleader of riots at Beaulieu Jazz Festival—arrested twice."

Linda was a girl of fourteen. She has already been mentioned in one of Bill's letters as the girl who was the subject of questions in Parliament. As she was being shown round the school she gave Bill one of those looks which he quickly realized said: "I'm used to dealing with people like you but I'll wait for a day or two before I start giving you the 'run round'." "You can get out if you like," said Bill replying to her look, "before we have too much bother with you. It'll save us a lot of trouble because just at the moment we've got a hell of a lot on our plate in other ways trying to get the new school going. But, you know, you might find that this is really rather a different sort of joint from any of the others you've been in." There was always just the right sort of approach for every individual child and Bill seemed to have the knack of finding it.

Derek, a dark-haired boy of eleven, arrived with two social workers. He'd played them up and he knew he had them where he wanted them. They wouldn't dare use force, he'd reckoned, and so he could treat them however he liked. Bill perceived that they were decidedly uneasy with him and were only too glad to hand him over so that the responsibility for what he did shouldn't rest with them. Bill did nothing to the boy except take him by the arm. Without showing it he deliberately gripped him like a vice. Derek didn't wish to show it either for his pride's sake. Again things were starting off in the right way. The boy had to regard Bill as a man. Bill gave him a square deal in return. Derek liked the general feeling of freedom and relaxation in the school but he didn't regard Bill as 'soft'. He had his angry moments and he even ran away once. Bill shot off after him in his Jaguar, taking a circular route which brought him back along the road on which the boy was departing. He grabbed him by the arm again and pushed him into the back of the car and returned without saying a word. For a few seconds he let fly at him when he returned: "What the bloody hell have you got to escape to, you stupid little so and so. If you get out of here they'll have you really 'inside' in the end. So you might as well stay here. You'll get a chance here but perhaps you're too bloody half-witted to take it." Bill then walked off in apparent disgust. He said things in this way in a desperate attempt to get the boy thinking realistically about the situation he was in in society, where he was labelled almost as a potential criminal. Derek settled down.

A little group of four very young children came next. Outwardly they were rather sweet and colourful toddling around the grounds. They were all under five and they strengthened the sense of having a real family in the school, especially for the older girls who were now arriving. The case histories even at their tender age made somewhat distressing reading. Bill felt that the myth of innocence should not be too readily exploded for very young children. They were left to their play and fantasy and to the care of Lillian and the older girls.

Elizabeth was the next big girl to arrive. She came fresh from the riots at the Beaulieu Jazz Festival where she had been arrested. Linda, who was by now settling down and had some clues about what the school was really driving at—at least enough to prevent her from running away—now had a companion. The presence of the younger children had given her and a couple of the other girls the opportunity to take up moral attitudes themselves. How righteous they could be! They even tried to infect other children with their opinions about how the young ones should behave. They hung round Bill like Victorian nannies asking questions to which the answers were implied and intended to make Bill mad with them. He turned his head sideways and looked at Janet. "Ah, shit," he said, and the look on his face was one of sheer and utter disgust. "Christ!" she mumbled as she wandered off, "headmasters don't say shit." His response had its effect. The morality at which he felt impelled to fling that comment was just one side of a coin. The other side was all the compulsive lavatory joking of repressed children.

Elizabeth proved to be no real difficulty. On Saturdays she and Linda would, in Bill's words, dress up like a couple of tarts and go off to town. One evening Bill made them look at themselves in the mirror when they returned. "There, what d'you think of that?" he asked. "Christ," replied Linda, "we do look a bit daft, don't we?" They began to soften down slowly from then on, and as they did so, to take more interest in the domestic side of things. They were still somewhat addicted to smoking, unfortunately, and Bill never tried to stop them altogether or at once. He continually pointed out that his main reason for being against kids smoking was that it usually forced them to steal. He didn't mind too much if they poisoned their insides or ran the risk of lung cancer but until they were old enough to earn a reasonable amount of money themselves he warned them to keep off 'fags' if they possibly could. If, as in the case of Elizabeth and Linda, he knew it was too much for the child to break herself of the habit at once, he weaned her (or him) by giving her the stub ends of his own cigarettes for a while. It may not have been a very hygienic practice but it had the advantage of causing the child's craving to become related to him personally. The child no longer thought of getting cigarettes from elsewhere. She would badger Bill and this Bill accepted as part of his job. It was like that with Linda. Elizabeth, fortunately, developed a much greater interest in domestic affairs. Her story will appear more fully later.

A couple of the children who had been with Bill at Alresford arrived and the group was beginning to fill out. One of the Alresford children had announced to his local authority that he would go to no other school than the one Mr. Malcolm was in charge of. He knew that Bill was intending to start up a new school when he left Alresford and he had implicit faith that this must have happened by now. As the group grew from its small beginnings Bill began by settling all problems on a personal level, between the children involved. It was his very close attention to the details of personal squabbles, always solved with an emphasis upon giving children insight into each other's motives, which paved the way to the meeting. I noticed especially at this time how deeply Bill was prepared to go into children's arguments and how hard he would press to find their causes. This was one of the distinguishing features of his work for it is in sharp contrast with the practice in most schools where there is so much concern over external justice. Sometimes he found that an element of temporary unfairness even helped some children to see into their own motives and drives. The fine distinctions which come into play when motives are questioned are often shirked in schools because they appear as a threat to the firm application of a system of discipline.

By the end of the first term the first school meeting was called. It was a simple affair in which Bill explained the idea of self-government and some of the positive things he wanted to try to do in the school. The children talked of some of the things which were done at other schools which they had attended and discussed especially the camps which they were anxious to set up in the grounds. As the meetings went on the children began to charge one another more seriously, developed a sense of what could and could not be brought up at the meeting and became steadily more responsible in their behaviour.

The two Andrews who at the time of writing are still in the school arrived during the Spring term. In his own way each added something of his own individuality to the school. One went round the school from morning till night dressed as a witch. He was quiet during lessons but paid absolutely no attention to his work. It was a slow business getting him related to reality and it was done only by letting him live out his fantasies and unrealities. He will probably never catch up academically with other children of his own age but he gets crazes which he follows up assiduously and has a strong liking for certain domestic tasks. He undertakes in his own time and completely voluntarily the regular task of keeping the vast floors of the present school excellently polished.

The other Andrew was a very different sort of person. He has a personality that is liked by all. He is never in any bother and never has been. He just simply couldn't stand normal schooling and broke down constantly under the pressure exerted to bring him to school. He was obviously intelligent and capable although understandably backward in some school subjects. He took a tremendous interest in nature and natural history from his very first days at Childscourt. He collected specimens and watched birds, kept animals and insects, and all with a real sense of purpose and an intense interest in life. There was no dark hate within him, making him want to tear the legs off insects when adult attention was turned away. He did not want to kill birds, destroy nests or take the unhatched eggs away. He was allowed to go ahead with his own studies and interests and was helped whenever possible. He was even given the exclusive use of a small room behind the kitchen, in which to gather together and arrange his material. "Why can't we do the same?" demanded some of the bigger, more aggressive boys. It was a wonderful opportunity for Bill to make them look into themselves and see the reasons why he made this distinction, why he let Andrew do these things and why he didn't let them. Andrew went ahead with the opportunities given to him without the slightest trace of falsehood or aggression. His motives were transparently clear: those of plain engrossed interest. Through the sheer simplicity of his manner he somehow managed never to make enemies. He was never involved in squabbles or fights and yet he was never thought of as soft or derided by even the toughest characters in the school. He provided a great deal of stimulating material for those early meetings at Long Bredy.

Thus as time went by the various children began to mould themselves into a happy, contented community. There were not such desperate characters among them as a few of those at Alresford, nor did quite the same criminal influences seem to be waiting to pounce on them when they went home or wherever they spent their holidays. The pleasant appearance of the school and the growing sense of assurance on the part of Local Education Authorities and Children's Officers that once they sent children to Childscourt their worries with them were over, led to expanding numbers in the school and eventually to growing waiting lists. This fact together with the demand of the Ministry of Education for extensive alterations in the sanitary arrangements if numbers in the school were to rise above twenty-five made Bill see that two possible courses lay ahead of him. Either he could go in for an extensive and expensive building programme where he was or he could look for a bigger and more suitable house. He chose to try to follow the latter course. After going up many blind alleys and after almost insuperable financial difficulties he finally managed to place a deposit on Lattiford House, a really splendid mansion in Somerset with a large ballroom which could serve as the school hall he was beginning to feel in urgent need of in order to develop dramatic activities, ballet and the other community projects which he felt to be especially necessary for deprived children from poor homes in our drab cities. At long last it looked as though the school was going to end up in the very embodiment of what Bill and the kids at Penybrin had dreamed of seventeen years earlier.

6

Childscourt—
Its Present and its Future

The move to Wincanton in Somerset was arranged to take place at the beginning of January 1963. One of the worst blizzards of the century swept the coast of southern England and isolated the little school at Long Bredy. The move was delayed for a fortnight. When Bill and Lillian did finally arrive at Lattiford House they found that the previous owner had completely run out of fuel and had been unable to do anything to prevent the whole central heating system from freezing solid. Almost every pipe and radiator in the house had burst. The children's return had to be delayed for a further fortnight but could scarcely be delayed any longer. The school was in complete chaos when I first managed to get down on a visit. Even the cold water had to be collected in milk churns from a tap in a field several hundred yards away and Elsans had to be put in the lavatories. Conditions were difficult but spirits were high. The day came, however, when the sun shone and the snow cleared and the school slowly began to function as a school once more.

The children who had been at Long Bredy had a strong nucleus among them who had gained some understanding of Bill's ideas. They had achieved a great deal of freedom for themselves and were becoming trustworthy, but they were still essentially weak. It had been clear to Bill that if they were to come up against a strong influence they would easily give way again. At the time of the move, however, financial and other pressures had caused Bill to accept four older boys, hardened in their ways and very typical examples of the worst results of 'c' streams or their equivalent in the Secondary Modern system. They were a challenge to Bill and even more a challenge to the children who came up from Dorset. The school could either be strengthened or broken by them. Bill didn't intend that it should be broken but he did know that their presence might retard some of the other children for a time. Once they had recovered, however, Bill believed that the school would gain additional strength and would prove once more its ability to cope with the severest problems that could confront it.

On my first day in the classroom at Lattiford House I felt in those boys the deep-seated insolence which is produced only by years in the mill of an educational system which fails to understand the child's refusal to accept it. One of the boys had been beaten in front of his class almost every day for two years and since this did not have the desired remedial effect his headmaster, in his report on the boy, assumed him to be of thoroughly bad and intractable character. On a pragmatic basis his procedure and assumptions are apparently justified. Most children do jump to it if there's a threat in the background. In the case of the minority who do not the 'culprits' merely become hardened. They grow accustomed to beatings and find compensation in the fact that the other intimidated children are prone to regard them as heroes. They gain power in their school and form a nucleus of hardened and irresponsible children (the exact reverse of what Bill had always aimed at). If those 'heroes' handle the power they gain clumsily they are labelled as uncontrollable. If they handle it skilfully they can succeed in driving weaker, and often more sensitive children into doing their 'dirty work' for them and bearing the burden of the consequent punishment. Torn between two harsh powers: the authority of the school and the threats of the strong children, many are unable to stand the strain and get themselves, for quite a different reason, classified as 'maladjusted'.

It must be stressed here that, contrary to a pretty widely held popular belief that corporal punishment was dropped in all schools after the 1944 Education Act and that the reintroduction of a little beating would somehow solve all the problems of delinquency, beatings are administered in most boys' secondary schools. In some this is done only by the headmaster. In others it is done according to the rules laid down by the Local Education Authorities. The authority to cane may only be given to teachers after several years of teaching experience (many a young teacher in an authority I know of personally has spent those early years hungering and thirsting after the day when he can take a cane in his own hands and beat the 'little brats' who have known their advantage while it lasted). Many of the cases which come to court and receive tremendous publicity are isolated instances of teachers, often genuinely at their wits' end, who have struck out without following the prescribed rules for inflicting corporal punishment. It is these reports which create the impression in the mind of a certain section of the public that children in present-day schools are regarded as little darlings who cannot be touched without a fuss in the newspapers.

That little group of older boys who had just arrived at Childscourt were real products of a system of beating. They snarled as they said things. They tried to catch teachers out in order to laugh at them, they indulged in orgies of destruction and organized others into their plans, bullying if necessary and possibly finding little pleasure if they could not do so. They had a crust, a very hard crust which had been built up over the years. It was this that Childscourt had to break through so that what was underneath, their natural characters, could become visible once more.

It is the policy of the school to eschew entirely all forms of organized corporal punishment. The basic motivation of such punishment is seen as being sadistic and perverted. It is also the policy of the school to avoid replacing it with a moralism which can do just as much damage to the natural development of children. The sentimental responses of moralism to the real tasks of educating children can come from sources no less perverted than those of actual beating carried out in a calculated, sadistic fashion. Bill is always

D

emphasising his belief that the reactions of a teacher should be the normal reactions of a complete human being, capable of being roused to anger on occasions, capable of irritation and impatience, capable of showing weakness but never guilty of putting on a false front for children just because they are children. There is a time for straight, clear reasoning and even a time for just saying firmly "don't". Bill believes that that is certainly the limit to which it should be necessary to go with the normal child, but when his emotions have become a furnace of raging hate the point is reached when nothing but raging hate will quell it.

Bill's problem in the case of these older boys was then a tough one. He could not appear to be offering them the other cheek. If he did that to them he would be offering them morality and sentimentality with all their inhibitive and provocative associations. He could not be punitive because that approach had already failed. The job had to be done through the meetings and the everyday life of the school. Bill comes into the meeting one morning with a despairing look on his face: "The 'heroes' have been up to it again—another one of their bits of senseless destruction . . ." and he launches into a tirade against senseless destruction and bullying. There is not a trace of admiration or anything that might stimulate admiration in a single word he utters. He refers all the time to the 'heroes' and by doing so he is striking the first powerful blow against their main source of strength. As if by accident, and perhaps without bothering to become fully conscious of what he was doing at the time, he was throwing the idea of heroes back in their faces and at the same time making the rest of the school uneasily conscious of their own tendencies to regard these boys as heroes. A discussion on punishment ensued. One of the big boys speaks up, but he speaks a little uneasily, "I think, Bill, you're too soft with us." Bill replies instantly, "Look, son, here we don't punish people until we have clear evidence. If I find you doing anything I'll act (and he puts quite a bit of emphasis on that word) and if anybody else finds you he should not be afraid to bring it up at this meeting. It'll take some courage because we know that you do some sly work on the smaller ones, but we'll find a way of protecting them and some of them'll have the courage to speak up. Anyway we're doing something different here from your other schools. We don't really believe in the constant, sadistic, brutal punishment which goes on in some schools. . . ." The subject was rather deliberately left in the air for Bill never sought instant solutions or put himself into a position where he would be committed to any piece of once-and-for-all punishment.

It happened at that moment that one of the teachers produced a book which she had discovered in the local library. It contained the history of Lattiford. There was the story of an old mill mentioned in the Doomsday Book, the story of a twelfth century chapel in the grounds of the house and the later story of the building and burning down of the house and its final restoration, as well as interesting snippets about its various occupants. The attention of the meeting had switched from a sordid, destructive subject to a discussion on Georgian mansions. This was something positive and Bill was glad for it surreptitiously to take the place of the negative things about which he hoped enough had been said to stimulate the processes of self-awareness and insight. In fact the meeting launched into a full-scale discussion on the possibility of an extensive project on the whole history of Lattiford and Wincanton when the new classroom block was finished.

With all the difficulties and disturbance it was hardly surprising that lessons went ahead on an ad hoc and somewhat disconnected basis. No real unity could be brought into the curriculum and no satisfactorily progressive basis for lessons could be laid. Every effort was made, however, to teach the basic subjects by up-to-date methods and the greatest stress was always laid on the development of the understanding of human relationships through the meeting and on the growth of children's power to express themselves, for Bill always hoped that they would grow up into the sort of children who could never be swayed by mass opinion or talked into a senseless pattern of life through advertising.

The frame of mind of that new group of boys remained really inflamed throughout the spring and summer. Only in the autumn, after much had happened, did it really begin to temper itself. Still it was noticeable how they began to shed the masks of behaviour bit by bit. Their attitude to teachers changed first. It began to dawn on them that there was no point in their show of insolence. Teachers at Childscourt were not, and did not have to pretend to be, horrified by their language or by pieces of behaviour intended to shock. There was no admiring audience for the young 'heroes'. Their performances fell flat and they knew it. They could only turn in anger to their destructive activities. They were heroes no longer. At best they had slightly perplexed spectators; at worst courageous opponents. The situation at this stage may be illustrated from one of Bill's own accounts of the school's progress: "All did not go smoothly of course; we had admitted nine new pupils in a short space of time and they were distinctly uneasy in an environment free from the pressures they were used to. They found that at Childscourt it wasn't even possible to gang up against the hated adult in the usual fashion of kids up against it; nobody of any importance in the group was interested. A few scuffles broke out when the more hefty of the malcontents decided to make their presence felt. When warned that they would be charged with bullying they grinned and when Raymond, aged five, bellowed that they would have to do what the meeting directed he was chased into the house. Raymond, who didn't appear to know the meaning of fear, brought the matter up at the meeting. This was the challenge, all the children knew it, and a hush settled over the meeting. The case was clear, bullying was disruptive and made everybody unhappy, therefore something must be done about it. Witness after witness got up to support Raymond and three of the hefty ones found the case proved against them, the sanction being to wash up at supper time for three days.

" 'Won't do it; can't make me,' bellowed one. This threw the ball right at my feet and without hesitation I supported the decision of the meeting as its first chairman. I had momentarily to forgo my principle of encouraging freedom of thought and action. If I allowed the challenge to pass because of my principle there would be no more freedom for anyone. The bullies would set the pace in the group. Therefore I said, 'We shall see that you do.' The meeting then finished its business and everyone crowded rather untidily through the door. I stepped in front of the belligerent Nick saying, 'Laddie, there is some washing up to do, do it now.' He looked quickly at his friends who turned uneasily away; then he muttered 'Why should I?' 'Because the meeting decided that you should do so,' I answered. 'You mean because you say so,' he snarled. 'No, I'm just going to see that you carry out the decision of the meeting,' I replied. 'Well,' he muttered, 'I'm off.' I gripped him by the back of the neck and directed him towards the kitchen. 'Keep your hands off me, you bastard,' he bellowed, 'I thought that no force was used in this school.' 'Yes, that is why you're here,' I said softly, 'now wash up.' For a long moment he stared at me, then slowly put the dishes in the sink and turned the tap on. I stood watching him for a few moments, then picking up a tea towel I began to wipe up for him. No further words were spoken until the task was finished and I let him go without another word.

"In the following meeting I announced that Nick had kindly helped me to wash up; and now we expected him and his friends to do the same at dinner time. Nick's friends looked at him quickly but he just nodded his head. After supper young Raymond came rushing into my room. 'Them boys is washing up,' he panted, 'and water is all over the floor.' 'Well, we have to be satisfied with small mercies, Raymond,' I replied, 'they will be all right in time.'

"All this did not of course entirely settle the matter; we had our ups and downs; but I can say now that Nick eventually found a centre of interest for himself and is now one of our most talented footballers and takes his full part in all school activities. Mind you, two and a half years have passed since that first challenge and the turning point came a few months ago when one of the younger children was charged with 'egging Nick on to bully by calling him Big Head and Mountain Man'. The accusation was upheld and the young offender was directed by the meeting to help peel the spuds. Nick then realized that the law which protected the weaker also protected the apparently strong."

At the end of the first spring term at Wincanton, Bill struggled to put on a special production of *Richard III* which he had prepared himself. It was a splendid historical pageant which took as its theme the idea that Richard was not the malicious hunchback he was reputed to be but a man of valiant nature who, when he was forced to the issue at Bosworth field, had arranged for the princes to be sent off to sanctuary until after his victory. Instead, of course, he was defeated (and being defeated defamed) and died seeing the treachery of bitter and evil forces. It is characteristic of Bill that he should have chosen this version of history not for any emotional reason but because, after comparing the portraits of Richard III and Henry Tudor, he saw behind the treacherous features and the little beady eyes of the latter the same kind of maniacal look that he had seen in the 'enemies' of children during the course of the whole of his experience in hostels and schools.

Drama also provided another good opportunity for the children to learn to speak out and express themselves. In the guise of others they could forget themselves and their own inhibiting problems for a while. It was an opportunity for them to experiment with the idea of being other people. Bill has always enjoyed historical romances and accepted them himself as an outlet at times from the tough life he had set himself to follow in reality. He has always been fascinated by the simple notions of loyalty and treachery and the readiness of men to boast and speak out their minds which one finds in historical romance. The same human feelings are still there today but they tend to be hidden behind the interpretations of a much more highly sophisticated psychology. It is naive to look at them directly. It is naive in our mediocre, rather grey society even to try to see things in their true colours.

In the plays which Bill adapts and constructs for use in the school things are not 'written down' for children. If anything they are written up. Behind the striding, swashbuckling knights, the sceptre-swaying kings, the queens and ladies of the days of chivalry, all of whom children love, lie the stories and problems of entangled human emotions. Anyone who has seen the absorbed interest of children in drama and literature when they touch upon the problems in the depths of their own personal lives will realize how much there is for children to take from this kind of play. Nobody is prying into their reactions. There is merely something that children can take from these plays. No one will watch how they use it. It will become part of their own inner education, a private thing.

Bill's own part in these school plays has been a matter of some controversy. He makes himself the centre of the whole activity. He has written the plays himself. He produces them himself. He takes the part always of the principal male character. He is the hero for the boys and the emotions of the girls are focused upon him. He believes this to be an important factor in the life of the school. He makes himself a substitute for the old gang hero worship among the boys and he believes that by keeping the emotions of the girls set on himself for a time he prevents them from forming relationships with the boys which they would be unable to control. He believes that it is only through doing this that he is able to keep together a group of emotional boys and girls without frequent pregnancies occurring.

As at Alresford, football was becoming another very prominent activity in the life of the school and again Bill made it have a very special bearing on the problems of the moment. He was always captain of one side himself but changed individual boys around from time to time. When things were going badly with the older boys, the real whereabouts of the strongest hates against authority quickly revealed themselves. Their disappearance too showed very clearly indeed. Thus it was not only a game which Bill himself liked but a way in which he could keep in touch with the emotional state of every boy in the school. It was never a conscious business of prying but it frequently enabled him automatically to know who were the real culprits, the prime movers, in any disturbance. I once heard Bill say to a boy who came up to him blaming some other child for something, "I'm not a bloody Solomon, son!" Sometimes, however, he seemed to get very near to using the ancient king's technique! A little change could sometimes give the boys concerned quite a jolt. It could help to break up whole constellations of thought, create the need to build up new and more sensible patterns of outward reaction.

At first the games on the new football pitch at Lattiford were very scrappy. Boys wanted to squabble over every little incident. A greal deal of self-control had to be learnt to make the matches resemble a game. It was evident how much the players needed to gain insight into their own emotions and this they generally did gain. It was the unintelligent clash of both inner and outer drives, which showed so clearly on the football field, that was at the root of all their problems. It is a self-destroying thing turned blindly in a kind of defence against powers they cannot understand, a fairy tale in which their own weakness and the strength of outside opposing forces are reversed. On the football field the boys at Childscourt needed to learn that they were playing a game and were not merely on the field to demonstrate their own prowess. The situation called for co-operation with other members of the team. At first boys were loath to pass the ball. All that concerned the boy who had it was to keep it and make one mad rush towards the goal. Of course he never got there. A sense of the need for co-operation was being forced upon them, not by any authority but by the nature of the social situation. Glory was only to be gained when you knew your own weakness as well as your own real strength.

Often Bill took the boys away from lessons for a number of extra afternoons' football. He was very apologetic to the teachers. "It's not just football I'm taking them for . . ." he would say. It sounded too much like psychology to give an explanation. The teachers had to understand. Gradually the game did change. "Things are beginning to fall into place," Bill would comment simply. The boys changed too. They were beginning to learn some of the simple lessons in self-control, lessons which they should have learnt at four or five, lessons which most people assume are learnt automatically. The young teacher who discovers this absence exclaims in amazement: "They won't even settle down to the things that they like!"

One of the big boys was to leave at the end of the summer term. He was of the age to leave but in a sense his departure spelt one failure for Childscourt, although it had to be remembered that he'd been at the school for only a little over a term. He'd become very helpful on the technical side and had run the school's cinema programmes singlehanded (a picture and sound projector was purchased during the summer term). He was already running a small radio repair business at home on his own account during the holidays and did really possess a very capable technical mind. He was obviously far above the age at which Bill would normally entertain accepting children but had unfortunately become involved in violent episodes at an earlier stage in his life, which had led him into a mental hospital where drugs were administered to him. He was freed from their effect while at Childscourt but unluckily made contact with an adult who was in a similar condition and had had similar experiences. This brought on an anxiety condition which it was clearly too late to cope with at Childscourt School.

There was another very disturbing case of a drugged child who arrived with a supply of drugs administered on a medical prescription. She was an older girl of somewhat ungainly appearance, a fact which lay at the root of her problems. People in despair take readily to any escape that comes to hand. It is often not realized how easily this kind of despair can operate in the sensitive period of adolescence. Drugs are the easy way out. In the case of this particular girl Childscourt was the ideal place where the environment was such—a controlled environment—that she could easily be accepted in it and feel accepted. Children did not work out any abnormal bitterness on others who were a little bit out of line either physically or in behaviour. That, of course, was largely controlled through the meeting, and Bill himself had a keen sense of when a particular child needed some protection. A little casual comment sometimes did the trick: "Don't take any notice of what she said to you, lass. She's nothing very special herself. You really don't want to worry about what she says and if she says very much more about it I'll tell her one or two things that could be said about her." A girl being criticised by others in that way might come back to Bill again and again. Every time her inward worry would become a little bit less, no dramatic change, just a little bit less.

The first job with the girl with drugs was, of course, to take them away from her. She could not participate in the life of Childscourt half doped. The task, in her case, involved telling her one or two strong truths about the people who gave them to her. Bill deemed it of the utmost importance to discredit them in her mind and was not afraid to do this. From then on she made quick progress. She soon found that Childscourt was not the sort of place where people pick on you and she soon began to take an active and genuine part in all the things that were going on. She was accepted.

She looked back only once. During the holidays after her first term at the school she was given drugs again in spite of Bill's firm request that this should not be done and when she arrived back at Childscourt once more she was in a semi-stupor. The process of undoing the damage had to start all over again and this was made harder by the fact that the return to the old method of settling her problems had cast some doubt on her own view of the progress she had made during the previous term. This was overcome, however, and she appears to be turning out to be a fairly capable, quite sensible child with a fair ability for academic work. She was merely rather more sensitive than many another child with the same sort of problems.

Clearly one of the chief elements in that girl's initial recovery was Bill's unshrinking and unlimited readiness to bring the doctor who had made the original prescription into discredit in the child's mind. Bill had slowly come to disregard the aura of demanded respect which surrounds the psychiatrist. He was now prepared deliberately to tear to shreds every vestige of authority which the children, although in revolt, also accorded to their psychiatric doctors. Bill found this to be an important part of his work and he continued to use this method when necessary at Childscourt. Anxiety was clearly relieved when in the child's mind the psychiatrist's approach to his guilty interior was discredited. "I'm no longer the nutty one and I might not be altogether wrong. The people who are prying and poking into me may be the nutty ones," was a new trend of thought which clearly brought immense relief from anxiety and guilt to many children.

One particular very anxious but very intelligent girl, whom I observed, showed an instant sense of relief when Bill remarked, "Ah, they're a nutty lot these people who go around prying into you. There's something wrong with them really." On another occasion I was questioning a boy from Southampton during a geography lesson and I wanted to see if he knew that Southampton had recently become a city. "Have you lived in Southampton all your life?" I asked and I went on plugging him with questions because I thought he probably knew the answer I was trying to get out of him. After a short time he turned on me accusingly and said, "You sound like a psychiatrist."

Bill's approach to children on the score of psychiatry may seem questionable to many people but it has to be remembered that it is the image of the psychiatrist and the side-effects of the close individual-to-individual relationship that he is trying to counteract. Dr. R. F. Balfour, Senior Consultant of the Child and Family Guidance Service at Bristol, speaking on 'The Child, the Family and the Psychiatrist,' recently emphasised the significance of the "unfortunate public image" which the psychiatrist had created of himself and went on to give a practical illustration of its significance: "Often when the question of a child being

107

referred to a child welfare clinic comes up the reaction is: 'He is not so bad as that.'" This is plainly an expression of distress and deep-seated fear on the part of the family, which is undoubtedly communicated to the child: he is, so they believe, assessed in the eyes of society as mad, nutty.

Barbara Wootton in a speech in the House of Lords already quoted is also concerned to give attention to some of the side effects of psychiatry: "After long experience in the courts I find that I begin to deprecate the perhaps too rapid recourse to psychiatry in the case of young people who find it difficult to conform to the laws and moral standards of the society in which they live. . . Children very quickly get to think of themselves as poor little things suffering from some disability, and the side-effects of attendance at a clinic, or of going to the doctor for apparently mental or moral feelings, are not entirely to be discounted." Barbara Wootton concludes: "I would perhaps be less inclined to mention this point if we were blessed with greater success in the kind of psychiatric treatment which is used for delinquent children. I cannot help noticing the contrast. In my lifetime there has been an enormous improvement in the treatment of certain diseases. Tuberculosis is no longer the scourge it was; the rate of infant mortality has fallen out of all recognition in half a century. But I notice that, although we multiply our child guidance clinics and the psychiatric services attached to our courts, there is no improvement at all in the figures of child delinquency: and I am a little bit inclined to judge all branches of the medical profession by the same test—that is, whether they do or do not, in fact, produce results. But that, my Lords, is the least of the dangers; there are others which are more subtle."

Returning to the school, we may continue to look once more at Bill's way of coping with the social problem just mentioned. One evening in the summer the children went out to the local cinema for a change and saw rather by mistake a film which would not have been chosen for them. It was a wartime escape story and included some very vivid shooting scenes by the Nazi Gestapo in a prison camp. It showed their jackbooted strut in all its realistic horror. Peter, one of the older characters who arrived at the beginning of the Easter Term, remarked in Bill's presence in the classroom on the following day, "Ooh, I'd like to be a Nazi." And he said it with real spontaneous desire. Bill rounded on him instantly: "Don't worry, son; you are one already." The only difference was that the Nazis were not in power in Childscourt, though it was not for lack of trying by Peter and his friends; and they never could get into power.

Still, the very presence of such wishes indicates the state of mind children can already get into, *in our society*, by the time they reach adolescence; and it is pretty clear that appeasement by sentimental and moral remedies is not a strong enough answer. In the present instance the boy had suddenly been brought up against a picture of himself. Bill had grasped a momentary opportunity to ram home another fact that might lead him along the path of self-awareness. And this kind of thing is happening the whole time. It is a community where teachers and staff as well as children are constantly brought up against themselves, for once the process starts on a social basis nothing can stop it and no one can be exempt from it.

The ideas and aims of the meeting were really beginning to sink in. As was mentioned a little earlier in Bill's report on the school's progress, the bigger children were even beginning to reach the stage at which they were considering charging some of the smaller ones when they took advantage of the protection of the meeting to egg them on.

Stephen was one of the old pupils from Alresford, who now had a job as junior staff, doing such vital tasks as helping to get the boys down to breakfast on time in the mornings and assisting with, and supervising, the cleaning up after breakfast, both down in the dining room and later upstairs in the boys' bedrooms. Bill liked it this way. Stephen knew from experience something of how things worked out at Alresford and his being not so very much older meant that the problems which might well have arisen if an authoritarian figure had been set among them were avoided. Perhaps it might have been different if there had been no staffing shortage and just the right person could have been picked for this delicate task among the boys. This idea of junior staff was to lead the way to solving the difficulties with certain leavers who were not yet ready to go out in the world and it was to become one of the distinctive ways of Childscourt for dealing with the potential problems of after care.

To some Stephen might have appeared to be in very much the same position as a school prefect. To Bill's mind the meeting made an important distinction here. Stephen had the responsibility of a prefect but not the power. On odd occasions when he was tempted to take the power the meeting decisively overruled him. In general he understood the function of the meeting and tried to lead and persuade others to use it as the following example will show. Today at the meeting Stephen explains how he had encouraged one of the older boys to use the meeting instead of his fists "on the school's prize little worker up, Barry." After some persuasion, Stephen explained, the boy had agreed to use the meeting for a week and if it hadn't stopped Barry by then he was going to revert to the law of the jungle. Bill grasped this opportunity to press further his explanation of the purpose of the meeting. "Look, Barry, I could go into action and stop you or anybody else in two minutes; so could David (the boy concerned); the meeting could also do it but, you know, it's not really the purpose of the meeting to punish you (this was directed at David who obviously wanted to use the meeting as an instrument of punishment). We want you to stop *yourself* annoying David. Why do you do it, Barry?" "I dunno, Bill." The latter was really quite a confession for a little boy to make publicly. It would undoubtedly start up a chain of thought in Barry's mind so the subject was deliberately left. "Why can't we have our camps and rations like we used to have when we were in Dorset?" asked one of the boys who had come up with the school when it moved. "You can't have them now. We've got a few little Nazis among us and do you know what they'd do if you were allowed to have your camps out of our sight?

Arms'd be twisted off and old friends of yours'd be trampled into the ground. You know the kind of thing I mean?" The "yes" of the kids from Dorset was accompanied by a faint nostalgic groan. "When we really trust the majority of the kids to use the meeting, you'll be able to do all those things again."

It was constantly being suggested to Bill that he should provide quiet rooms for the over-thirteens. There should be somewhere where the older children could get away and be by themselves. It had even been said that, when he was at Long Bredy, he was wrong to have the bushes around the grounds bulldozed away. "They made such a lovely place for children to play without being watched by adults," one visitor commented to me. I do not know whether such people merely fail to realize the quantities of pent-up aggression in children who have recently come from desperately harsh environments or whether they feel a need for a natural toughening influence to be exercised by the school community. There is no doubt that in the days of Nelson and Wellington the violent conditions under which the poor lived provided the soldiers and sailors who could really fight wars, but in general the conditions of the modern world no longer require society to provide such a school for warriors. At any rate at Lattiford Bill gave way to the suggestions of visitors and pleas of the boys for a 'quiet room'. Quiet room it may have been for a short time but not for long. It was situated away from the main part of the house and it was only a matter of a few days before the savage impulses of some of the boys, fighting and arguing with each other, as they had earlier been doing on the football field, one supposes, finally broke most of the furniture and put their fists through the ceiling in several places.

"I'd like to keep this place as a museum—a museum of destruction," Bill remarked to me as he showed me the devastation, "it merely shows the absurdity of giving children such facilities until they are sufficiently settled inwardly to use them for their proper purposes. You can't explain this to most people though. They think that they know what these boys should have but most of them are judging from their

111

own experience and do not see what these children are really like. I must admit that they do look pretty settled to the casual observer, but we know that they've got to be prepared for whatever is given them and that it takes a long time with some kids."

Back in the same meeting in which the question of Barry had been brought up, Mrs. ———, one of the teachers, now wanted to bring up the girls she'd taken out to games on the previous afternoon. "Yes, I know," said Bill, "I heard a hell of a row going on and I saw both the boys and the girls making real fools of themselves. As you know I couldn't get out myself and some dim-witted boy hung on the goal post and broke it." Bill doesn't hesitate to bring their intelligence into question when they do stupid things *which he knows they themselves know to be stupid,* or to refer to them as 'sub-human' when they have done vicious or brutal things. Far from damaging their security, as some might fear, these concepts seem to enter naturally into the children's own thinking about their behaviour and widen their capacity for self-criticism. "There was some trouble around the outhouses, I believe," exclaimed Bill in the same meeting, "well, what was it?" A reply came at once from one of the older boys, "I was going to try and knock the slates off that old shed near the dump but I thought it would be a bit sub-human so I didn't." "Anyway," Bill went on, "you just went crazy outside and if you go on like that when you're just out of our sight we can't trust you to behave reasonably when you're at the pictures. Now that's reasonable, isn't it? I've looked through the list and there seem to be about four people whom we can really trust to go on an outing to the cinema. We'll let them go but we'll have to stop the rest."

Another emergency meeting was called the same afternoon. This was something that happened very rarely, only at times of crisis and disturbance. St. Valentine's day was approaching and there was some excitement among the girls who were making a bee-line for a boy who had just arrived. The way in which they did it seemed fraught with danger and worried Bill. "It's one thing for boys and girls," he started in an irate tone of voice, "to be normally friendly and live together on good terms in a community like this, but when a 'new pair of pants' comes in you all set upon him until he doesn't know what's happening to him. There'll be no limits to what he thinks of himself after you lot have been at him. He won't even be able to think properly. Quite a good trick for reducing a male mind to pulp! Anyhow I've told him to keep away from you and if he doesn't he'll be kept away from the school and that'll settle it. I prefer the 'louts' and 'heroes' with all their destructiveness to this sort of thing. They've got a bit of hate in them and they want to get it out somehow. What you're doing is something that can destroy a kid on the very first day he comes here. You've got your 'pop' dances in the evenings. I've let you have that as an outlet and if you want any more you'll have to wait until you leave here. I couldn't let you have more even if I wanted to or we'd be shut down by the education authorities within a week. But, in any case, you're not going to turn this school into a bloody nightclub. It's got to be a place where boys and girls can live together normally. Well, after this tirade, you'll probably behave a little more like human beings for a bit—until the effect has worn off."

There was a generally chastened atmosphere among those present and Bill felt that it would not be out of place to change his mind about the cinema visit. With the exception of one or two children, who he knew would cause real trouble, they could all go. Threats were often not carried out, for Bill felt no need to create an authoritarian image of himself. There are few dramatic punishments at Childscourt and few harsh orders are given. There are warnings for first offenders, mitigating circumstances are always taken into account and punishment when it does come is usually very light but it does carry the authority of the community. Most anti-social attitudes are worn away by gradual attrition. You never actually see them go but every now and again you suddenly realize that so and so is quite a different child from what he was a couple of terms ago.

E

113

Great changes are wrought by the environment and the interaction of personalities. Bill has always, of course, believed that if there is a sound nucleus of children in the school, who live and act intelligently, their influence will quickly be decisive on every newcomer. He had proved this to his own complete satisfaction at Penybrin. He knew also that until this nucleus had formed and had become strong and free from many of the influences in outside society, it would often be necessary for him to step into and cut across the processes of self-government and take instant and sometimes apparently high-handed action. But he works on the principle that such action must only ever be taken to protect the community's growth towards genuine self-determination. It must never be merely an excuse for returning to authoritarianism. The nucleus of children who are learning the meaning of freedom simply have to be protected from near Nazi influences. This social factor lies at the core of Bill's work.

In the majority of schools the brunt of discipline is borne by individuals. The mob influences are never really chastened, never brought to heel and almost any school teacher of experience can verify that, with even the worst classes if he has individual children helping him clearing up or doing some other job after school, the individual child can change into a pleasant reasonable person within minutes of leaving the group which inspired his bad behaviour. The mob hypnotizes, draws, thrusts into violent action, and over-rules the individual's mind and conscience. To achieve effective law and order it is necessary to get to the source of these powers. It is no use dealing with the manifestations alone. When the shackles of civilization and morality are taken off, human beings reveal themselves for what they are, as the boys do in *Lord of the Flies* and as children do at Childscourt. It is then that one can see and deal with the real situation.

Bill may often seem to be doing nothing much to individuals, but all the time he is using the meeting and the various activities of the school to modify and suppress this

114

tremendous mob power which so often goes unchecked or is even stimulated by the kind of punishment administered. Its victims become the victims of the law. Delinquency is automatically multiplied and the real sources of criminality escape untouched. When this mob influence is checked, as it is at Childscourt, intelligence and sensitivity can enter into human relationships.

While I was writing this chapter the day's *Guardian* (19.5.64) arrived reporting the activities over that Whitsun. It reported: "Fines of £50 dealt out again and again by the magistrates for 'threatening behaviour whereby a breach of the peace was likely to be occasioned' shook the boys visibly, caused their waiting girl friends to weep and drew some gasps from the police who arrested them." I wondered why gasps should have come from the police. In my own mind I was prepared to hazard a guess that it was probably because they knew in themselves that it was only a matter of chance whom they had managed to arrest. They almost certainly wouldn't have got the moving spirits of such violent mob behaviour. The root of the matter was not tackled and by sending many young people to detention centres and even prisons, they were probably merely creating another crop of criminals.

It is not severity of punishment that will check the rise of delinquency in our society but the extent to which we are able to uncover its real sources and deal with them. The problem should already have been tackled in our schools and yet we can read in such a book as *The Insecure Offenders* of children sitting in their classrooms in London dreaming of the day when they can get away from it all and join the local gang. *The Guardian* gave what seems to me the right answer, at least in very general terms, when it concluded its leading article on the subject by saying: "Theirs is an ailment which can only be cured when the places in which they live and the schools in which they learn are less cramped, less frustrating and less deadly to hope." Childscourt, I believe, gives the same answer but in much more specific terms.

If you were to go to Childscourt now, the door might well

be opened by a rather short, efficient, tidy and attractive looking young girl. She would be pleasantly polite but not subservient to you. You would probably think that the school was fortunate to have such a pleasant, efficient young girl on its staff. "Where do they get young people like that today?" you might ask. As the school progressed, Elizabeth, mentioned in the last chapter, who had not so long before been sent to Childscourt as a pupil when the school was in Dorset, after being arrested by the police (not for the first time), for being at the centre of the disturbances at the Beaulieu Jazz Festival, had now at scarcely seventeen become one of the most capable members of the staff on the domestic and house-mothering side. She did not merely do a lot of the work. She also did a great deal of the domestic organization. Arrangement of laundry, getting in of dirty clothes and distribution of clean ones after she had washed them, was only one of her tasks. The interesting point is that she did not have to be told how to set about it; she worked it all out herself with the children. Lillian frequently remarks with amazement how methodical Elizabeth is: "She has a far better mind for organizing than I have. I can be quite sure that if I leave anything to her it will be done efficiently and on time. I don't know what we'd do without her now." And yet the answer to where she came from is: from the rowdy teenagers at the Beaulieu Jazz Festival! She might equally well have come from Clacton, Brighton or Margate. It was probably a mere chance that she was sent to the place that had the right answer for her. Thousands of others must have gone to the wrong places.

In the autumn of the school's first year at Wincanton a full scale three-day inspection was conducted by the Ministry of Education. It was a fairly successful inspection and the inspectors were highly complimentary in their remarks concerning the initial success in setting up the school and the good human relationships achieved in the community. In discussing this inspection it must be remembered how difficult it is for the casual observer to gain any idea of what is really happening at the meeting at this stage of its development. With the more mature group at Penybrin the situation was quite different and visitors were inevitably impressed. But during the early stages many of the meetings at Childscourt could seem extremely unimpressive and ineffectual. The reason for this was that Bill did not aim to turn them into an effective court for punishment. Sanctions were administered not as firm deterrents but as part of a process aimed at giving children insight and self-awareness. To an outsider what was said often looked like sneaking and a penalty of merely peeling spuds for trying to burn the school down might look like grossly inadequate discipline. But in fact the meeting could never be viewed in terms of punishment or discipline. The child can do, and does the same thing he has been charged for today, tomorrow and on many tomorrows. But the day comes when a change comes from *within the child himself.* It comes not from a single stern order but like the growth of a seed in nature.

One of the inspectors told me that he was especially impressed by the helpful attitude of the children. He gave me an example of what he meant: on the first day of his visit he lost his way as he was walking between the classrooms. As a result he asked a girl in the corridor how he could find his way to a particular teacher's room. She showed him the way quickly and politely and left him immediately, he told me. He was surprised by this because, as he explained to me, in almost every school when a child does something of that nature for you, he or she leaves you with a feeling, be it ever so slight, of expecting or faintly hoping for something in return. The Inspector concerned regarded himself as having become extremely sensitive to that kind of feeling for, as he pointed out, he had had plenty of opportunity to do so. He felt no trace of such feeling from the children at Childscourt and regarded it as a significant indication of their emotional progress.

It has often been said that "Bill and Lillian simply had a way with children" but I hope that by now this book has at least begun to make it clear that there were distinct reasons for the responses of the children with whom they dealt. There was little point in complaining that there was no clear-cut authority over the children, for the care with which the traditional type of authority was removed was itself one of the reasons why the children made such good outward progress. Behind that façade, which was very necessary and served an important function, was the long-drawn-out tug-of-war between the staff and the children. That was where the real work of character development went on and anything that implied a denial of that work or impeded it was contrary to the principles on which the school was fundamentally based.

An example of this occurred during the inspection. One evening when most of the children had gone to the cinema in town one of the inspectors returned and visited the dormitory where Lillian was putting some of the younger ones to bed. A few items of their clothing were lying around rather untidily. The gist of the inspector's response to this was: "They must be *trained* to fold their clothes and put them tidily on their chairs. The importance of training at this stage cannot be over-stressed. Even blind children can be trained to do these things in an orderly and tidy fashion." She went on to describe this being done in a school for blind children, which she had inspected. Lillian was savage and suggested that the inspector herself should try to 'train' these children and see what happened. She felt also that it was wrong to compare them with blind children. Blind children get their interest in life from accomplishing tasks which bring them back nearer to normality. Folding their clothes could be an interesting challenge for *them*. For the children sent to Childscourt folding their clothes, or rather being trained to fold their clothes, would represent the kind of discipline which they hated and revolted against and which in fact had failed to control them. They simply had to find their control from within.

The fact that Childscourt is as orderly as it is (and most visitors remark, in the general context, on the orderliness of the school) is due to the fact that it does relax the children

118

and leaves them free to develop a sense of order in the tug-of-war just mentioned. The fact that observers often misunderstand what is happening does not mean that they should be criticised. They are almost bound to be misled by the children's good exterior which masks the real emotional problems which lie at different stages of partial solution beneath the surface. I think that no one could help unconsciously applying some of the standards he would apply to above average children.

Another incident during the inspection will illustrate this point. In the afternoon before the children went to the cinema I was wandering round the school with the inspector with whom I had been talking earlier. We happened to meet one of the big boys who by now will have become rather notorious in this book. The inspector asked him the title of the film he was going to see and then proceeded to ask him the meaning of a word in it. The boy, who was in any case rather intelligent, gave him a very short, simple and extremely precise definition. The incident caused him to comment to me immediately afterwards that it was important to ensure that such a bright boy had the full advantages of an advanced education made available to him. This of course was true but it was not the boy's first need. On the spur of the moment I doubt if that inspector realized the boy's underlying emotional instability. Only during the previous holiday (he had only been at Childscourt since just before Easter) he had got himself into several bits of severe bother for stealing and it had been all that Bill could do to save him from being sent to a detention centre. Of course his education was important, but it was a matter of priorities and there was something much more than academic education to be dealt with first. Little good advanced education would do him if he had to waste away his days in prison. If, on the other hand, he could be steadied up emotionally there could be little doubt that this particular boy, an avid reader of a good range of books, would find his own way towards advanced education and make use of the facilities available in adult education. If Childscourt tried to push too much into him at the wrong time and didn't succeed in steadying him up he might well find his way to a 'Clacton' or a 'Margate' before getting round to advanced education.

Nevertheless Childscourt does have several teachers with university degrees and other well qualified staff and is providing courses leading to C.S.E. in a number of subjects and it is hoped to widen the range as time goes by. It is important to ensure that this does not inadvertently lead staff to put on pressures which may be disruptive emotionally. The comment of the psychiatrist of one of the counties which send children seems much more realistic. Referring to the children his county were sending he remarked, "If you can make them a little happier and balance them up a bit and teach them a bit of reading, writing and arithmetic while you're doing it, you'll be doing as much as anybody should reasonably expect you to."

Bill wants to do more, of course. He wants the children who go out from Childscourt to be able to think about things for themselves. He wants them to be fearless and courageous about questioning everything—but not because of a chip on the shoulder. He is certain that children who have been to Childscourt will not be afraid to speak out and up in front of others. The meeting will have 'trained' them for that! They will do it naturally and take it in their stride. They will never be like the semi-articulate, almost totally illiterate, disgruntled masses who fill the lower echelons of our vast industrial machine. Bill is confident that their lives will never be limited by that terrible inner emptiness which makes many a modern worker no more than a lifeless cog in the machine of modern society. One symptom of this Professor L. A. Reid refers to in *Philosophy and Education* (Heinemann, 1962) as: "a loss of a sound sense of personal individuality in the face of the tremendous drive to social conformity." It is just this "sound sense of personal individuality" that children at Childscourt gain. It is this, I believe, that prevents them from being driven into pointless, unconstructive, anti-social behaviour.

To this extent Childscourt provides a small sample of the

answer to the overwhelming problems of delinquency in modern times. It shows also how it can put the boys and girls who come there on an emotionally and intellectually upward, instead of downward, path. For crime is surely bred from conditions, sometimes even affluent conditions, which lead the young to depression and despondency. Childscourt gives to all its pupils the background of a home with verbal ability and real powers of thought.

In these days when the cry for harsher measures for dealing with recalcitrant youth is fairly familiar to us all, it is surprising that more attention is not given to uncovering the real inciters of trouble. The real spirits behind mob violence may well need much more violent suppression. And if we do not get the real sources of trouble and still use harsh measures we are liable to embitter and turn into criminals a very large number of merely high-spirited or misunderstood teenagers.

It must be remembered that in protecting children from the Law, Bill has been doing no more for the children from lower class families than fathers from richer families have done for centuries to protect their sons whose behaviour at university rags for example would otherwise have led them to jail. This protection does not mean that Bill is 'soft' with children. He can be ferocious at times. Peter, our 'Nazi', was on the football field one day. He suddenly took it into his head to administer a really vicious kick with his heavy football boots to one of the small boys on his side. He was angry that a goal had just been scored against his side. Bill instantly tore into a ferocious rage, got him by the back of the neck and almost threw him off the field. He roared at him to get right off. For a moment Peter thought of resisting. He snarled back a 'no' from the other side of the field and Bill turned on him again. Peter almost screamed like a cornered animal as Bill approached him. Twice more he tried it until at last he was standing over the boundary of the field. His vicious will was beaten in this encounter. It was not, of course, the end of all trouble from him but if Bill had not done this at that moment he believes that Peter would have felt himself free to establish his own vicious dictatorship amongst the children.

Such methods as the foregoing, Bill realized, were contrary to his ideals but a society in which freedom is being developed must protect itself against those who demand freedom for themselves to operate tyranny. Too many ideals in education never become realized because of a weakness inherent in the ideals themselves, which prevents those who are trying to build up a better sort of community from taking the necessary action to ensure that it is not destroyed before it is properly built.

Many other steps taken at Childscourt in its present stage of development look like denials of freedom, and those who stand for freedom complain and those who tend to stand for authoritarian trends approve for the wrong reasons. The camps have not yet begun again. Bill does not yet trust the children to conduct their own play while one or two 'Nazis' are about. It may seem unfair on the others but he wants them as a group to see those isolated boys for what they really are and cope with them themselves, not by violence but by making themselves immune to their influence. Boys and girls at present play in different parts of the grounds. Bill is usually quite straightforward about giving his reasons for this. An example will again illustrate his approach. Mary came into the sitting room one day (she had a record of severe nymphomania according to the psychiatrist of her county) after watching a programme about a co-educational school on television. "It was very nice," she said, "the boys and the girls were all allowed to be friends with each other." "Very nice idea, lass," commented Bill, "but I can tell you what would happen if I let you do that just now. . . It would, wouldn't it?" "No, it would be all right, Bill." "Would it? I know what would happen. I might as well put up the red lights outside if I let that happen now. Later on it'll be O.K. but not just yet," and he let her give him a kiss as she went off to continue looking at the television in the girls' sitting room.

It may seem surprising to some that a whole school can

wander almost at will into Bill's and Lillian's own rooms. Children are usually expected to give a knock but the doors are almost always open. Sometimes a child is turned away but only as he might be in a home: "Lillian's just having her tea. Don't disturb her now. Give her a few minutes' peace, son." "O.K., Bill." Even their own bedroom, which is situated among the girls' and small children's dormitories, suffers constant invasion during the day, except for Thursday mornings, which is Lillian's day off, when it is thoroughly understood by the whole school that she ought to be allowed to have a lie in. Nowhere is closed to the children *on principle*. They are sometimes stopped at particular times for natural reasons which they really understand.

"It's good," Bill says, "when they just come in and talk naturally. Soon I hope we'll get a group like the one at Penybrin. I can talk to them then about the things we're really trying to do. If only a few intelligent ones can appreciate the kind of community we're really driving at and really want to enjoy its advantages, it will completely change the whole atmosphere of this school, on the inside as well as the outside." Such conversations do occur when Bill is working in his classroom in the evening or when a few of the kids edge their way into his sitting room or over a late night cup of cocoa in the kitchen.

It might seem to some that such conversations are bringing Bill very near to psychiatric interviews. That, however, he would strenuously deny. They are never direct discussions of children's inner problems and he claims to avoid any personal interaction on the doctor-patient level by getting the interaction operating between the individual and the community as a whole. Bill certainly makes no conscious endeavour to alter anything in their inner lives. He aims to inspire children with a social ideal, and to make them aware of how easily they can make themselves victims of some of the harsh forces in our present society. He aims to give them a positive *external* reason for seeking the kind of self-discipline and sense of responsibility that will leave them free without bringing either themselves individually or the school as a whole into trouble. There are many signs that this sort of ideal school community is being slowly achieved but it will be some time before a community like that at Penybrin is achieved. In its simplest terms this endeavour is merely a way of trying to find a thoroughly practical solution to the age old problem of the philosophers: the conflict between the individual and society.

For the end of term and the first Christmas at Wincanton the English teacher, a specialist in drama and elocution, produced Marguerite Steen's version of the Pied Piper of Hamelin. She set about the task with the thoroughness that would have been required for a really high quality performance—and in the final result she achieved it! But for many of the children the strain was unfortunately too much and there was cursing and swearing and "I'm not going to do it for her, etc."

Bill's was a more flamboyant approach, designed to appeal to children still very much at the 'cowboy and indian' stage of their development. Bill steps into the leading part and hires the most expensive costumes he can get from Nathan's in London. The kids not only learn their own parts but often large chunks of other parts as well. The play, *Camelot*, which was being produced at the time of writing, is Bill's own adaptation of the Arthurian legends as presented in Philip Lindsay's novel. Once again Bill is in amongst the children as their leader. They feel this and feel the expense of the costumes. "This one was used in such and such a film." "Ooh, was it really, Bill!" For these end of term events Bill reckons that the very considerable sums of money spent on these costumes are by no means wasted. As is the case with some of the extravagance of the furniture it helps to make many rather disgruntled parents feel that their children are not being fobbed off with the cheapest in education. Every time he can make them feel a little swell of pride he knows that he is getting them on the side of the work he is trying to do for their children. He believes that one of the most harmful influences on the development of these children comes from a feeling on the part of the parents that their children are among the rejected, the throw-outs of society.

It must be obvious that the school's attitude to the curriculum and to school organization must continue to be experimental. There are many factors to be borne in mind before applying the normal pressures of our educational system in this school. Nevertheless the experience at Alresford convinced Bill that completely 'free' lessons for these children were not a good idea, and he was impressed by the fact that the freedom of the hostel in Wales had caused the children to do well in conventional education. An up-to-date account of the curriculum is to be found in a report, included at the end of this chapter, by Pat Goldacre, the school's present Head Teacher. It may merely be stated at this stage that the problems of arranging classes with such a wide age range and the likelihood of emotional incompatibility are proving almost insuperable. Providing a satisfactory range of subjects to satisfy the demands of a modern curriculum is difficult in the smaller secondary schools with several hundred children and they are now tending to be no longer regarded as viable units. In a school of fifty children covering infant, junior and secondary levels the task is well nigh impossible. It is still hard to see how these enormous difficulties are going to be overcome and yet for full recognition it is demanded that such a school should provide facilities comparable to the best standards in secondary education.

Bill himself likes many of the 'extra' subjects to spread outside the timetable and be integrated in the life of the school. For the girls domestic science means helping with the running of the school—joining in with the domestic staff to help with the cleaning and the cooking. The boys help with maintenance, decoration of the school and gardening and no distinction in principle is made between the teaching and domestic staff. The children know them all by their christian names as they do Bill and Lillian. It seems to those at Childscourt better than learning cooking in an artificial way. It makes the children's work part of the

125

real work of the community and they can identify with adults in the same way as boys who go out with their fathers fishing or hunting in a simple society. We believe that there is a little bit too much stress on 'child centred' education these days. The essential forms of education in all simple societies are distinctly adult centred and the whole process is attuned to the idea of becoming adults. The motive to learn seems to spring from this idea.

The attitude of Childscourt to examinations is, I think, interesting. In view of the matter of fact attitude towards the basic skills it is hardly surprising that the school finds itself unable to object too strongly to marks, tests and examinations in themselves. It is felt that most of the harm is done by the attitudes associated with them, particularly those built up in children by nervous or over-ambitious teachers and parents. If a child feels a desperate need to pass exams and too much depends on them they are certainly harmful. If on the other hand a child feels that they are something in the nature of a game—a fairly serious game— they should do no harm at all and be useful and encouraging to both teachers and children. I can recall end of term exams at Childscourt from which the children came out making such remarks as: "That was rather good fun, that was." "It was like a quiz, wasn't it?" "I think I really quite enjoyed that." The general competitive attitude towards work is minimized. Cheating for instance is never taken very seriously and very often a couple of friends working together can do much to fill in gaps caused by frequent absence from their previous schools. It will be some time, however, before the real academic pattern of the school can be expected to emerge.

Material improvements are going ahead on all sides: a new classroom block is in process of construction behind the house. Two excellent football pitches, with shining white goal posts stand over beyond the gardens—and form the playing fields of Childscourt. A tennis and netball court as well as an asphalt playground (laid by some of the older boys) with swings, slides and sand pit for the younger children have just been completed, and a swimming pool is on the list of possible improvements for next year but this like the rest of the story lies in the future.

Apart from a few general reflections this brings my account of the Malcolms' work and the formation of Childs-court School to an end. I am aware that it has been sketchy and anecdotal but I hope that the sketches and anecdotes cohere and build up into a sufficiently complete picture to convey the real importance of the work going on there. By the very nature of the school and its methods it has been impossible to give detailed and systematic coverage of its development or a series of fully documented case histories to prove its success. But perhaps that is not what is really needed in education. I believe that a great deal of research in this field is far too detailed and lacks a sound sense of proportion and of practical application—'Training College stuff' as it is sometimes referred to by busy teachers with an element of truth. I would like to write of the significance of the work of Childscourt as William James wrote of the work of a friend of his, saying that it showed, "a sense for the perspective and proportion of things (so, for instance, you *don't* make experiments and quote figures to the 100th decimal, where a coarse qualitative result is all that the question needs) . . ." (*Letters of William James, Vol. 1.*)

Nearly two years have elapsed now since this chapter was originally written and a new, brief look at the school is needed. Materially a great deal of further progress has been made. New books and new teaching equipment, especially for the younger children, have came into the school. The new classroom block has long since been finished. Two additional attractive classrooms with beamed ceilings have been made out of the old rooms in the annexe, which the boys destroyed. Bill has established his own classroom as a real showpiece among classrooms. A complete stage has been constructed at the far end of the big hall—the former ballroom of Lattiford House. The attic over the stables has been converted into a magnificent 'Art Barn' where painting, modelling, etc., take place and where a continuous exhibition of the children's paintings is on display. A new handicrafts room in the house, near the centre of things, has been set up and is run by Lillian, providing for the whole school, particularly in the evenings, what she had long ago provided for Jimmy and Bob in Cornwall. The great entrance hall to the house and Bill's own sitting room which is immediately adjacent to it are grandly furnished with antiques. The immediate impact is one of traditional wealth and splendour and this Bill considers to be of considerable importance in raising the whole status of the work being done in the school from the level of back alley charity to that on which the upbringing of children of a great nation should be. This impression helps enormously to establish confidence in parents who come to the school with the feeling that their children have been rejected. Bill feels that he can say, "Here your child gets the best education," and gain credence for his claim.

Several of the older boys who caused so much trouble at the beginning of the time at Wincanton have now left. Unfortunately their careers in several instances have not been successful. The work of Childscourt cannot be done in a few terms and it must be remembered that Bill has always insisted that the work must be begun between the years of seven and twelve. From this Bill has developed the idea of a 'junior staff'. None of the children can stay beyond fifteen or sixteen at the expense of the local authorities but now towards the end of their time Bill keeps a close eye on the leavers who he thinks will get into trouble if they are pushed too quickly from the relaxed environment of Childscourt into a foster home where moral, religious or other pressures bring about a reaction. Such children often are excellent workers in the right environment and when somewhat more established after earning their own living at Childscourt will be ready to face the outside world. Their numbers have now risen to half a dozen and their work ranges from that of Elizabeth, already mentioned, to that of Harry who works with the gardener to keep the grounds trim as well as tending several large greenhouses and over two acres of kitchen garden.

Since the departure of those older boys Bill reports that the atmosphere among the children has become distinctly less harsh, and steady progress towards a sound nucleus of children is evident. It is obviously a much harder thing to achieve here at Childscourt with fifty children than it was with twenty odd in one of the hostels in Wales. Nevertheless numbers are essential to sustain the staffing and other provisions necessary for the running of a school which is co-educational (thus having to supply the needs of both boys and girls) as well as covering all stages of education from infant to secondary. Furthermore Childscourt pays its way and is not dependent on charity for a penny of its income.

Perhaps the biggest recent change has come on the educational side. The school needed a really good Head Teacher. It needed a person thoroughly acquainted with modern methods in education—as the Inspectors had said—and with a bit of organizing wizardry to fit together subjects demanded by a modern curriculum, time available and teachers with some assumed limits to their capacities! Also it had to be someone with an ability to co-operate really sympathetically with Bill's aims and methods. Pat Goldacre had exactly these qualifications. She had, apart from degree and teaching certificate, experience of teaching children of all ages, was an admirer of A. S. Neill and had worked for some years as a reference librarian which had given her varied experience of the world outside schools. The following account by her on the present work of the school does much to bring this story up-to-date and provides interesting indications of the lines on which it may be expected to run in the future:

"The problem I was faced with was that of organizing a satisfactory education for fifty children—usually twenty-five boys and twenty-five girls—of ages ranging from five to fifteen, of broadly average intelligence, with I.Qs within the range of eighty to one hundred and thirty and with varying degrees of emotional disturbances.

129

"While these children, like all children, are highly individual and different, one from another, the one thing that most of them have in common on arrival is their attitude to learning. This is one of rejection and it is often expressed in two ways, either that they don't want to learn anything because nothing we teachers can tell them is likely to be interesting or useful, or else they don't want to be taught anything because they know everything that is worth knowing already. These latter are known among the staff as 'world-beaters'. The exceptions I would make to this generalization would be firstly the younger children of five to nine who are either extremely apathetic or wildly overactive and secondly a few of the older children who are ready to learn as long as they are nursed along emotionally. This pre-conceived attitude to learning is important because we take in a number of new children each year as vacancies occur and most of these are in the age range of twelve to thirteen, the children whom it has not been found possible to contain in their new schools after going on to secondary education.

"These attitudes of rejection, however, are often shown to be superficial and defensive within quite a short space of time at Childscourt, if we succeed in building up their confidence and if we can remove their sense of failure everyday in class. As one girl of thirteen said to me on her first day in one of my classes, 'I'm stupid, of course I'm stupid, or I wouldn't be here.' When I pointed out to her that this was not a school for stupid children, she said, 'Well, I'm here because I'm more trouble than all the other thirty children in my class put together. My teacher said so. But I'm really adorable, aren't I? My boyfriend says so.' Whatever else they feel, most of our children feel that they were a failure scholastically in their old schools, for the simple reason that they have been 'sent away'.

"The school is arranged into seven classes or groups, with six in each class and seven in one of the classes of older children. There are six full-time and five part-time teachers. The teaching staff give generously of their marking and preparation periods to helping children with special problems and the benefit of this is great. Children who are endlessly troublesome when anyone else at all is present, become teachable when alone with the teacher, and the really valuable thing is the way this change is carried over into the class situation later. Once this communication has been established in the new teaching situation, it does not disappear when the child returns to the classroom. So it is not necessary to give these special tutorials to any child indefinitely.

"When I first came to Childscourt I found that the classes were arranged according to attainment, not age, and were given names such as IA, IB. A tendency towards the processes of selection had crept in without anyone noticing it! Now we name the groups after their class teacher, such as, 'Rhona's Class', 'Mollie's Class', 'Pat's Class', 'Madie's', 'Mr. May's' and 'Mrs. Ruthven's'. The younger children, roughly of primary school age, are in co-educational groups, but Bill found that this did not work with the older children, especially with a sprinkling of girls who displayed a desperately eager and anxious attitude towards all boys. So the older children are arranged into groups of girls only and boys only. We regret this, because we would like to be completely co-educational, but with these children it seems to be the only way *at this stage*. I have arranged all groups according to age, primarily, with a two year spread, although the age ranges can sometimes have a one year overlap, e.g. 11–13, 12–14. Measured I.Q. or attainment are not usually taken as criteria, but emotional factors sometimes are. When we have brothers or sisters with a one-year age difference, we usually find it impossible to contain them in the same class. Sometimes a pattern of competition, bullying or championing has been too firmly established to be easily changed in the classroom and with these sometimes violent children these patterns can make teaching impossible.

"The older children are offered a course of study which includes the following usual school subjects: English, Maths, French, Science (with a bias towards Human Biology), History-Geography, Civics, Religious Knowledge (with a bias towards comparative study and without any moralizing),

Typing, Art, Handwork, Music, Sewing, Woodwork and Games. Of course we are very precisely limited by the abilities teachers can offer. Versatility in our teachers is very important in such a small school. One gap which I had to fill myself was music and I insisted with more than usual persistence that it should be integrated into the curriculum. The results have been good. I am not against pop music, but I do believe that it sometimes has a neurotic hold over children and I believe that this has been loosened as they become aware of other kinds of music. Our children have responded tremendously well to listening, to watching School TV music programmes and to class singing. The mechanics of writing music fascinates some of them in the same way that chess, shorthand or mechanical sums fascinates some children. I was very pleased that I could still play the piano sufficiently well to entertain my classes. Some love Bach, some Chopin, some Beethoven, but most cannot bear Brahms or Debussy. This surprised me. They respond to Benjamin Britten's *Little Sweep*. But I long ago gave up predicting either class or individual tastes.

"In a closed community like ours, in the heart of the country, school TV broadcasts are a window to the wider world and we watch suitable programmes. It is important to avoid watching anything that is over the heads of a particular group, or all TV school programmes are labelled 'boring' and 'no good' and condemned for the next few weeks.

"Over the past year we have admitted three West Indian children. We have had no difficulty in integrating them into a boarding school. I find that discussions in my Civics classes now tend to come back again and again to the question of race and these discussions seem necessary to the children. For one thing, many of the children do not seem to understand that skin colours are inherited and do not come by chance. In trying to explain this, I co-operate with our Biology teacher. In fact, although we teach separate 'Subjects' we try to convey a sense of the 'Unity of knowledge' and to build links wherever possible.

"The teaching of these children can so easily lead to

apathy on the part of teachers, as they become disheartened by the difficulties, frustrations and negative responses they encounter in their pupils every day, that it is especially necessary for us to bear in mind exactly what we are trying to do in teaching them the usual school subjects at all, why we at Childscourt attempt a rather more academic education than is often offered to children in special schools. As with any children, we are trying to help them to equip themselves to earn a living or to follow further training; to enjoy their leisure; to understand and cope with the confusing modern world; to acquire some power of expression and communication; and to develop the ability to tolerate and live peacefully with other people of different backgrounds and ideas. In everyday terms, when teachers are constantly called upon to act, this means having a suitable answer for the boy who says, 'What do I want to learn this for? I'm going to be a dustman when I leave school.' (He did not become a dustman, but joined the 'junior staff' and asked me in the kitchen one evening if he could join the teaching staff, because he'd always fancied being a teacher, he said!)

"The boys play football all the year round with Bill. The girls play netball and tennis. Because leisure time is not greatly organized, we have phases of great enthusiasm (as children always will do, given the freedom of opportunity and non-organizing adults) for table tennis, skipping, five stones, rounders, marbles, crochet and chess, which last perhaps a term and are then forgotten for a time. This moving from one obsession to another as a method of learning has always appealed to me. I remember how much my own children learnt at home in this way, following their own interests without adult interference in all their free time for years on end.

"In spite of all that I have written about our aims, I am bound to say that I see a great deal of truth in the story of the Inspector at Alresford, impressed by the children who were polite and co-operative only because they were talking to a visitor. It is indeed not as easy to 'train these children to take a progressive series of lessons in all school subjects,' as this inspector would seem to think. We attempt it knowing our limitations. We attempt a few C.S.E. exams with those children who are old enough to qualify for entry. Three at a time is the most that I have so far thought our boys and girls should cope with. Our results have been scattered over all the grades from I to V. The children have always been thrilled with even a couple of grade Vs. It is a wry pleasure for those of us who do not care for the attachment of great importance to examinations to see these children savouring the feeling of being 'like other people'. Those children who continue to reject 'a progressive series of lessons' are sometimes the more delightful personalities and, given a chance, could lead just as happy, useful lives as those who have their C.S.E. grades. Nevertheless, unsure of exactly what the outside world has to offer them, we suggest to the children that a certificate or two might prove useful sometime. The psychological uplift is certainly useful.

"You have read about a psychologist who wrote to Bill of the children, 'If you can make them a little happier and balance them up a bit and teach them a bit of reading, writing and arithmetic while you're doing it, you'll be doing as much as anybody can reasonably expect you to.' This is commendably realistic as regards a lot of our results. But at the same time, openly to aim low is to say to the children, 'We think you are pretty hopeless.' They know what goes on in the other schools. If we opt for teaching nothing but the 3Rs, we would be turning out children at 15 or 16 who were very underprivileged educationally compared with most other people in the community. That as we know would produce its own emotional problems.

"Of course there are many things which we would all like to do but have not been able to so far. Perhaps they will come in time. I asked the Department of Education Inspectors who came on a one day visit two terms after my arrival at Childscourt for their comments and advice on the overall organization of the scholastic side. 'Carry on as you are doing,' they said. I was very grateful to them, because as the reader may now realize, one receives a great deal of contradictory advice from the experts."

7

Some General Conclusions

Finally it seems to me important to restate a few of what I consider to be the main conclusions to be drawn from the work of the Malcolms over the years and end on a note conveying "a sense for the perspective and proportion of things". It seemed to me also that this should be combined with some mention of the relation of these conclusions to a few of the major trends in educational thinking. At the same time I wish to avoid too specific application of any aspect of the story of Childscourt to any branch of education or the upbringing of children or teenagers. It seems to me preferable at the moment that the story should be left to stand in its own right—simply as a plain account of the facts—though I believe, for instance, that a very interesting comparative study of Secondary Modern schools could be made against the background of the principles and methods used at Childscourt. I believe it would show that delinquency trends were much less pronounced where to some degree the tolerance and good sense of Bill's approach operated and much more prominent where harsher, more rigid and less understanding attitudes prevailed. I believe that this was the meaning of a remark made by a probation officer, which I recently heard: "We always know the schools from which the majority of troublemakers are going to come. . ." The main points to be considered, from which misunderstanding could easily arise, fall under four main headings: the attitude to religion at Childscourt, the attitude to morality (including punishment), the attitude to psychology and the application of 'common sense'.

It is essential to get the school's attitude towards religion properly in focus before the conclusion of the book. Childscourt is not in any sense anti-religious. Bill himself believes that religion has such tremendous power over the minds of human beings that it can arrest the development of natural thinking processes as well as the processes of adjusting to society in the young and can cause fixation of infantile levels of emotional growth. This is obviously dangerous and one would expect it to be deplored by religious and irreligious people alike. The recent work of Dr. Ronald Goldman seems to point clearly to this danger and where emotional disturbance has begun there can be little doubt that the problems can easily be magnified by the drastic implications of religious belief. Religious concepts, too, can easily confuse the undeveloped mind struggling to formulate its own necessary concepts to deal with ordinary everyday life.

At Childscourt, however, no child is prevented from undertaking any religious practice he or she wishes to undertake individually, the story of the life of Christ on earth as well as stories from other religions are read to the children during the course of normal lessons and every opportunity is taken by Bill to discuss the philosophy of life and religion. But no outside pressure is allowed to force the children into religious observances against their will and no actual act of worship is imposed upon them in the school. It will surely have been made fairly clear through instances of individual children mentioned in the story that exaggerated guilt and anxiety can magnify emotional disturbance rather than cure it. Other children, who under the pressures of life have had to become pretty smart to survive, see a pretence of being good, nice and religious as a very serviceable screen behind which malicious practices and really bad character traits can develop. Luther once said that man's most terrible crimes were all committed in the name of God. Let children grow up naturally and freely without any hypocritical observance, let their minds develop on the subject matter they can, and have to cope with and when they are mature they can decide for themselves what meaning religion has for them. This is the policy at Childscourt.

The next point, that of morality, is a very closely related one. To the moralist it may seem that some of the behaviour of both Bill and the children is peculiarly lax. Firmness and rigidity is not always the best way to achieve desirable moral goals. The taming of wild horses is achieved by knowing how much rein to give them and when. At Childscourt no moral generalizations are preached at the children. Specific instances of behaviour become stressed as acceptable or unacceptable to the community during the course of meetings or school life generally. Children come to form certain ideas about behaviour in connexion, for instance, with ways of treating other people, cruelty to animals etc., but they do not live under threats or a sense of threats and they do have real participation in the formation of necessary laws. One feels the children as a really powerful social group who know that they can make their will felt. No one will crack down on them for some piece of misbehaviour they cannot help. Smoking was a good example of that. Bill dealt with it gradually and kept the problem always above ground. Perhaps the distinguishing mark here is the fact that motivation is always taken into account and often discussed in remarkable detail at the meeting. It is not just a matter of punishing boy x for crime y. The community is confronted with the total setting in which unacceptable acts occurred and sometimes the inspirer—the egger-on— of a crime may be punished much more severely than its perpetrator. In this way one sees the community getting at the roots, rather than at the superficial manifestations of antisocial behaviour (and from this one of the most interesting lessons for dealing with our modern problems of delinquency may be drawn: if you punish misled, confused and weak people and don't get at the real inspiring spirits you don't deter crime, you create an additional race of criminals).

Perhaps the most important thing of all is the fact that Bill does not keep up a moral front for the sake of the children though of course it may be suggested by some that the moral tone of the school must be extremely low when the headmaster swears in front of the children. In fact this is not the case. There is an evident honesty and frankness among the children and matters of swearing and mint and cumin morality generally are reduced to their appropriate irrelevance and almost totally forgotten about. I was recently asked by a former teacher of one of the boys in the school how he was getting on. I replied, "Quite well," which was true. "But does he still have outbursts of foul language?" I was really rather bewildered by this emphasis and only muttered a rather weak and unconvincing "no". In fact he doesn't, but it was a rather odd question to crop up against the Childscourt background and I didn't give the firm reply I probably should have given. Society finds different standards (and double standards) for its various groups of people: one for the solid professional man, another for the actor and the artist and it is strange and incongruous that it should come to choose for its children, its weakest and least developed members, the morality of the saint to set the standard. It is surely the societies which have demanded the highest standards from their little children, which have produced the greatest crop of hypocrites: Judaism in the centuries preceeding Christ, Puritanism and Victorianism in more recent European culture.

To many the most confusing of all the attitudes taken up by Bill and by the school must be that towards psychology and psychiatry. In an age when mental health is regarded as being as much a symbol of progress and prosperity as the motor car or the jet aeroplane such an attitude may appear to be extremely reactionary. It is important therefore to define exactly what Bill is against and what the reasons for his opposition are. He is certainly not against the major discoveries of psychology during recent times. It should be evident that many of these are implied or even expressed in the extracts given from school meetings or annual progress reports. On the other hand it is also evident to those who know Bill that his attacks on psychologists and psychiatrists are not founded on any personal basis. As I have discussed the matter with him at length I have come to see that the individual doctor-patient relationship, especially in connexion with children, is the core of what he is opposing. He feels strongly that children should be influenced by a group or community as a whole and in a fairly open way, not by an intense enclosed relationship. With hidden or unconscious fears of madness in the depths and recesses of the minds of so many, Bill sees the intense relationship as a way of enforcing a particular morality on the young, which he passionately believes to be the wrong way of tackling the problem. He believes that our problems with our young will be solved by facing the rottenness of so many of our social institutions and widespread social attitudes, and not by individual psychotherapy so long as these remain unchanged.

T. R. Fyvel in his *Insecure Offenders* (Chatto and Windus, 1961) expresses what I believe to be exactly the same point of view. After visiting an apparently enlightened Approved School and speaking to its headmaster, he commented: "It seemed to me that his plans all concerned improved psychotherapy, while his problems all derived from greater *social* disorder." In a miniature setting, it seems to me, Bill is illustrating how to create a social order that will not produce the problems and he rightly sees psychotherapy as a danger to this approach, since its tendency, as it is today at least, is towards adjustment to the existing social order. The question of extending the categories of mental illness was mentioned at the beginning of this book and it is perhaps the heart of the matter against which Bill is revolting. The horror of a creeping social conformism is a spectre we cannot ignore even though to reveal it is often to court disaster for our own cherished careers. In her speech on this subject Barbara Wootton also expresses herself strongly: "After long experience in the courts I find that I begin to deprecate the too rapid recourse to psychiatry ih the case of young people who find it difficult to conform to the laws and moral standards of the community in which they live" (Hansard,

4. 7. 62). Confusion arises, I think, in connexion with psychiatry because some of its side effects, which are not very evident and are only realised after long experience, have the opposite effect from those of its expressed aims, which are undoubtedly worthy and widely supported.

It is hard to define what is meant by common sense but it does appear to have some kind of ordinary practical meaning which all can recognize. It appears to signify some sort of counterbalance to hasty theorizing which has not been refined by contact with the stuff that it is supposed to be about. It is this sense of long everyday contact with the stuff that the work is supposed to be about that is always in evidence at Childscourt. There is a pragmatic, on the spot sort of attitude, which one senses is right, but which is not always clearly related to the broad theoretical basis of the school's work. Bill frequently expresses this as "being prepared to step out of line from one's beliefs." He is prepared to do what is plainly the sensible thing in the circumstances to keep the school going on an even keel. This gives a real sense of control in the school but Bill believes that it operates to protect freedom and the fundamental rights of children, rather than endangering them.

There is a pretty widespread feeling that in many spheres of life today this sense of control has somehow slipped away. Even in football, I learnt from a recent account in the newspapers, there are complaints that refereeing has gone mad and referees cannot control the situation. In an interview with a journalist a well known former international referee made this comment: "But if I couldn't talk down trouble when it looked like starting, then I thought I had failed in my job." There seemed to me to be a lot of "old-fashioned" common sense in this remark and it struck me at once that it was just what Bill always did. He nosed out trouble before it had started. It must be faced *when it looks like starting*. It is then that one discovers its real instigators.

Much has been said about how Bill changed the attitudes and behaviour of the children who were sent to him. Evidence of this was found in the follow up of the children who were with him in the hostels in Wales. Unfortunately administrative difficulties made it impossible to trace all, or even a representative proportion of the successes of the children who were with the Malcolms at Alresford, and Childscourt itself is still too recent a venture for it to be possible to examine the successes of children who after being there for a reasonable length of time, have left and established themselves in the world.

Perhaps I have concentrated too much on the negative side of the work, the bad social attitudes and patterns of behaviour Bill has managed to overcome and get rid of, and not said enough about his positive vision. It is too late to rectify this but a short quotation from a book Bill sent me as a Christmas present a couple of years ago may help in this direction. I think it expresses exactly what Childscourt endeavours to prepare the ordinary child for, and somehow manages to cover rather magnificently the way in which it sets about this task: "For the first time in history the common man steps on the stage. We insist that education is primarily concerned with the ordinary person, and not with the exceptional person. The ordinary person is asked to decide issues of far greater gravity than any exceptional person in the past . . . When I complain about our schools imitating the public schools it is because they have a different task to perform . . . In order to be on terms of equality with the product of the public schools they must be trained differently. They are already too much inclined to obedience. What we want from them is more arrogance, freedom from the trammels of tradition. These boys and girls are asked to wield the royal sceptre; we must therefore give them the souls of kings and queens. Otherwise it may be said of us that we took the ordinary man from the shadows of history and set him in the fierce light that beats upon thrones and he was blinded and ran away." (*Aneurin Bevan, Vol. I*, by Michael Foot, Gollancz). I do not think that this will ever be said of children who have been to Childscourt.

Index

WHISKIN'S WORDS OF WISDOM...

"It never ceases to amaze me how hard it is to do a bit of good. Turf wars between agencies and departments, cumbersome decision making processes, resistance to change, finding and managing the money and so on, tough going. Sometimes, it really gets to me when those who could and should don't say 'yes why not'. We all want to do a bit of good and make life better for the people living in our poorest communities... At the end of the day, management-speak about quality assurance, continuous improvement, staff development and all that, comes down to being able to do good better - and to do better good."

"First, we frequently find ourselves between a dog and a whole avenue of trees. Because we work with youngsters at risk, our projects get criticised by some as being no more than 'treats for cheats'. 'It is not fair that bad kids get all the attention and good kids get nothing.' 'It's rewarding bad conduct.' But the difficult kids often won't use mainstream facilities where they exist and when they do, the parents of nice kids complain. So there is a strong case for projects for at risk youngsters."

"No one disagrees that we need protection from those offenders whose conduct poses a physical threat to us or whose persistent offending threatens to destroy the quality of life for the rest of the community. But the success of projects that target burglary 'hot spots', the Youth Inclusion and Mentoring Programmes that reach some of the most at risk youngsters in our most disadvantaged neighbourhoods, prove that prevention is better and cheaper than prison."

"Even if the police were better at detecting offenders, the courts dealt with criminals quickly and we had the capacity to lock up more prolific offenders most crimes would go undetected and most offenders not imprisoned. To ensure success, we need more investment in crime reduction and community safety in our most hard pressed neighbourhoods with crime problems to get real long term cuts in crime levels and reduce the number of offenders."

"We are still a nation transfixed by courts, cops and corrections. We don't really believe in prevention, reduction and creating safer communities. We don't really believe in community alternatives. We don't really believe we can change the way we deal with crime or the way we deal with offenders. We must always aim our work at the common sense, fair-minded majority."

"Listening to the debate at a conference on finding alternatives to custody, I was struck by how the arguments have not really changed that much over the last 15 years. It is about the tension between punishment and effective sanctions and the need to reduce the use of prison. The argument is long on rhetoric and very short on practical solutions!"

"We can look back over the last fourteen years with some considerable pride and point to the contribution we have made to innovation in crime reduction and community safety."

Nigel Whiskin

146